DEVELOP A BEAUTIFUL MIND GOD'S WAY

WORDS OF INSPIRATION AND AFFIRMATIONS TO
FREE YOUR MIND FROM WORRY, ANXIETY,
NEGATIVE THOUGHTS AND ENCOURAGE A POSITIVE
THINKING MINDSET.

EUNICE ONODE

I dedicate this book to my husband, Collins, and my children, Osede, Itohan, and Ofure, for all your love, help, support, and encouragement always. Most importantly, my sincere and heartfelt gratitude to our Heavenly Father for His love, grace, and guidance during the writing of this book.

just for you!

A FREE GIFT FOR MY READERS

Download *"How To Eliminate Negative Thoughts God's Way in 5 Simple Steps"* and start renewing your mind right away! Visit this link to get your free gift

www.euniceonode.com

CONTENTS

INTRODUCTION

---

*Every situation in your life that seems irreversible can
be reversed by the Word of God. Declare the Word!*

— PASTOR MENSA OTABIL

God's Word is powerful and can turn around any messy
situation in which you may currently find yourself. The
state of our minds often affects how we pray and the
results we get. A mind filled with negativity, worry, anxiety,
and fear is what I refer to as a messy mind. God's Word
has the power to make a chaotic mind beautiful and
bring beauty out of a chaotic situation. God is faithful to
His people and His Word. Applying God's Word to our minds

and circumstances can overcome negative, toxic and anxious thoughts and develop a beautiful mind in us, which puts us in a position to receive from God, and I can testify that God's Word WORKS. As an example, I want to tell you just one out of the many stories of God's faithfulness in my life.

When I was a young stay-at-home mom, and my husband was a graduate student, we lived on the upper floor of a small apartment building. Our neighbors who lived below us used to be disturbed by the noises made by my three-year-old and one-year-old children, especially during playtime. They would repeatedly bang their ceiling, which was my floor, to indicate their displeasure. I was at a loss trying to quieten my children, and this was causing me to be stressed out. We looked for another place to move to, but we couldn't afford anything else. I found the situation stressful, and I became anxious and worried.

One day, I felt the Lord prompt me to believe Him to provide for our need for a new home, so I started to affirm the Word of God to negate fear, worry, and anxiety. The wonderful thing about declaring God's Word is that it builds up faith in your heart for great miracles. I felt my faith grow and built up each day as I proclaimed God's Word, and then I began to act in line with my faith. This meant we had to be prepared to move any time. So I started packing up some things we rarely used into boxes and set them aside so that we would be ready when it was time to move. Every time my husband and I saw the boxes, we affirmed God's provision and thanked Him as our provider.

A few weeks later, an old acquaintance we had only met a couple of times, many years ago, arrived in our city for a visit. This couple knew we lived in this city but could not locate us even after inquiring, for they did not remember our full names. It was a short visit of three weeks and only three days remained when they were finally able to get our number from a mutual friend.

They called us immediately and asked to see us. We gave the couple our address, and they visited us that very evening. After exchanging greetings, they were intrigued by the boxes we had placed in the living room corner and asked if we were moving out. Then we told them about our unhappy neighbor and that we were believing God to move to another house, preferably one with no neighbors below us. We enjoyed the rest of the evening chatting about many other things, and when it was time, we wished them farewell, and they left.

The next day, the couple called and asked us to visit with them the same day as they were leaving the country the following day. We were at their place when the man asked us if we liked the house they were staying in, and we told them it looked warm and inviting. That was when we learned that it was their home and that they wanted us to stay there. They offered it fully furnished and rent-free for as long as we wanted as we were looking to move out of our apartment anyway. All they needed was that we maintained their house well. We were overjoyed. God had not only met our needs most unexpectedly but also provided more than what we ever asked or thought. God had given us a lovely house set in a convenient place and was very cozy, and we didn't have to pay any rent!

We stayed there for six years, which enabled us to save enough money to put a down payment on our first property. I could tell you many more stories of God's faithfulness so that you can be sure that God's Word WORKS!

Why did I tell you my story? I wanted to show you that you can develop a positive mindset using God's Word. Everyone of us can have a messy mind full of chaotic, negative, and toxic thoughts that most often spill out of our mouths when we speak.. After being saved by receiving Christ into our lives, we know that our spirits are renewed, but our minds remain messy, negative, and unrenewed. God has a solution for cleaning up our negative, chaotic, and messy minds and making them beautiful through His Word.

So I would like to assert that this book is not just another book on affirmation or positive thinking but one that enables Christ's power to become evident in your life. Books on Positive thinking have littered the marketplace because people believe in the power of positive affirmation. Merely saying positive things to try and strengthen and build yourself up on the inside fails because it is based on your abilities and falls short of its intended goal.

This book is grounded on the Word of God and the affirmations in it are from the Bible and personalized because God's Word is meant to be customized and applied to your personal situation. It is intended for the Christian man or woman who wants to speak what God says over them daily and those who want to rely on God's ability instead of their own and need God to help them overcome their weaknesses in life.

This book will help you overcome negative thoughts, clean up your messy, chaotic mind and help you develop a beautiful mind as you affirm God's Word over your life. It will help you think as God does because God, Himself, invites us to think like Him. In Isaiah 55: 7-9, we see that how we think differs from how God thinks, that is why God asks us to take His thoughts and make them our own. We can rest assured that His thoughts can become ours because God has written them down for us, and He invites us to read them and learn from Him because His thoughts are higher.

Reading this book –Develop a Beautiful Mind God's Way – will build up your faith to overcome any condition or situation you currently encounter. You are a daughter or a son of God, a child of the King, and God has already blessed you. Please do not use the chapters and affirmations in this book to beg God to do something/anything for you. Instead, they ought to remind you of what He has already done and of God's eternal goodness towards you in giving you many promises to claim as yours. Your part is to declare them with your mouth and then receive and enjoy the blessings of God. Every time you proclaim God's Word, you renew your mind and strengthen your faith in Him until you fully build up your faith to download the heavenly blessings.

HOW TO USE THIS BOOK

There are 13 chapters in this book. At the end of each chapter is a list of affirmations taken directly from the Bible, which you can use to declare God's promises over your life and situations. God's Word is the final authority, and God always honors His Word. He said in Isaiah 55: 10-12 that His Word will not return void but will always accomplish what He sent it to do.

Speak His Word in faith and confidence in a loving God. He will open up the wellspring of life inside you so that you can overcome every circumstance and situation in which you may currently find yourself using the power from within you. The Word of God works ALL THE TIME if we stay with it, keep our faith in the Word, only affirm what God says, and eliminate every other thought or Word which is not in line with His Word.

The audiobook version of this book has a five-second spacing after each affirmation to allow you to repeat it to yourself. It isn't sufficient only to hear God's Words, but it is also critical to speak them out of your mouth. Repeatedly listening to and speaking God's Words helps strengthen you, increase your faith, clean up your messy, negative, chaotic mind and develop a beautiful mind in you.

I chose the chapters in this book to cover several aspects of our lives where we most often have issues to deal with every day. The first and second chapters let us know who we are in Christ and then discuss the importance of and the power of God's Word in a believer's life.

The chapter 'Big Dreams and Visions' will encourage you to dream big because you have a big God who is more than able to fulfill your vision. We all have to deal with messy and negative mindsets, so the chapter 'Overcoming Thought Battles' will equip you to fight negative thoughts and win, using God's Word. The chapter 'A well and healed body' will help you know, or confirm what you already know, that it is God's will for you to walk in divine health. You will realize that healing and wholeness belong to you right now.

God's will for you is to be blessed so that you can bless others. When you read the chapter 'The Table is Prepared,' you will realize that the blessings of God encompass every area of your life. As people of faith, we must live by faith. The chapter 'A Life of Faith' will refresh and strengthen your spirit while encouraging you to use your faith to overcome different areas of your life.

Gratitude and Thanksgiving are an essential part of your spiritual growth, so the chapter 'A Grateful Heart' will encourage you from a biblical perspective to engage in the practice of gratitude. We all need God's help in various areas of our lives. The chapter 'Help and Guidance' will reveal how much God wants to help you if you let him. The chapter 'No Fear Here' is bound to help you rid yourself of fearful thoughts and find total peace of mind no matter the situation in which you presently find yourself.

Prayer is a very essential aspect of the faith life, and the chapter 'Lord Teach us to Pray' will show you that God is never far from you, and this understanding will change how you pray. You will go from a position of waiting to get your prayers answered to quickly receiving what He has already provided after you pray.

The chapter 'A Place to Dwell' will encourage you to abide in Christ so that your Christian walk can be effortless, just like the branch that stays connected to the vine produces fruit effortlessly. The last chapter, titled 'General Affirmations,' shows you the reasons why you should affirm God's words every day, followed by a list of generalized affirmations.

May the eyes of your understanding be enlightened as you read. Enjoy the book, and God bless you. Amen.

1

JESUS IS YOUR IDENTITY

"Our identity is not in our joy, and our identity is not in our suffering. Our identity is in Christ, whether we have joy or are suffering."

— MARK DRISCOLL

Scripture Reading:

"When someone becomes a Christian, he becomes a brand-new person inside. He is not the same anymore. A new life has begun!"

— 2 CORINTHIANS 5:17, TLB

Identity Crisis

From the time we are born and through the rest of our lives, we are in a quest for our identity. We find that even little children become curious about their bodies and who they are. My friend's three-year-old daughter asked her mother one day, "How come I cannot stand up and pee like my brother?" Children become aware of their genders and how little girls are different from little boys.

As we go through different stages of life, we begin to identify ourselves based on our skin color, community, race, history, nationality, profession, and so on. A young man might introduce himself as, "My name is Phil; I am from the USA, I am Caucasian, and I am an engineer." This journey to discover our identity continues even as we grow older because how we perceive ourselves might continue to change throughout the different stages of our lives.

How we identify ourselves varies from person to person. While some people identify themselves by what they achieved in their lives, others may relate to the remarkable things they have done to help others. Still, others define themselves by their physical appearances, such as whether they are tall and handsome, beautiful, graceful, fat, skinny, short, and so on. While all these ways of defining ourselves may be accurate, they do not paint a true picture of who we really are.

This search for one's true self often leaves a person feeling disconnected from life. We think and feel there is more to life than we have experienced thus far. Some people begin to experience midlife crises at the middle age of their lives, even though they may have been very successful in life, career, and business. Such people try to fill their emptiness or void with sex, power, money, alcohol, drugs, etc. Though these things help them for a short while, they do not provide lasting fulfillment for them.

We often feel disappointed when we try to seek real fulfillment from other things apart from God. He created us to live in a relationship with Him; as such, we can only find the satisfaction we seek in the life of God. It is like the lock and key analogy where the correct key can only open the right lock. In the same way, your Spirit can only open the door to who you really are by being connected to God, who is the very source of your life.

Your New Identity

Your profession, achievements, physical appearance, or wealth do not define who you are. When you come to God through Jesus Christ, He becomes your identity. The Scripture says that when you decide to become a Christian and accept Jesus, you become a brand-new person in Christ. Such a person has never existed before (2 Corinthians 5:17). Your physical body may look the same, but your inner man, your spirit man, is brand new. From that moment on, your unique nature is in Christ, and He is now your identity. Deciding to follow Christ changes everything and brings you into your true identity. You become one with Christ, and you come to know who you really are by seeing yourself as He sees you.

Most of us identify ourselves based on what we have been through in life. For example, people going through a challenging situation may have low self-esteem or a negative self-identity because they see themselves through the eyes of the situation they are going through.

Similarly, a sick person might see and identify with his sickness. If you have lived all your life in lack and poverty, you may identify yourself as poor. People generally define their lives by the condition they find themselves in or the environment in which they were raised. But the Scripture says you are now a brand new person in Christ. God says; let the weak say I am strong (Joel 3:10), so do not associate yourself with your former status. God does not want you to identify with your unfavorable conditions but identify yourself with who He said you are in His Word. As a Christian, you need to remove all negative self-identity that restricts you from embracing the beautiful new identity found in God's Word.

God sees you as a Spirit being like He is, and God wants you to know that you too are a spirit being just like Him. He wants you to replace the concepts that defined you before coming to know Jesus with a new identity based on who God is and what He says about you. You are one Spirit with the Father—the same Spirit that raised Jesus from the dead dwells in you right now (Romans 8:11).

How God Changes Your Identity

I would like to illustrate the concept of our new identity with an example. We read the story of how Abram used to see himself as childless as he could not produce an heir despite being married for over 50 years. In Genesis 15: 2-3, Abram was preparing to leave his inheritance to his servant, but God stepped in to correct Abram's identity so that he could see himself correctly and be able to receive the promise. God says about

Abram: "No longer will you be called Abram; your name will be Abraham, for I have made you a father of many nations" (Genesis 17:5, NIV).

God had to step in to change Abram's self-identity of being a childless man. So from the moment God changed his name to Abraham (meaning Father of many nations), he started to identify with his new name and identity. This was key to his seeing the blessings that God had promised him to come to pass.

Like Abraham, God has given you a new identity through Jesus Christ. Your negative self-identity may be that you think of yourself as not handsome or beautiful. You may see yourself as broke and poor, or infirmed and sickly or not attractive and bad-tempered. Whatever the negative self-identity that you may currently have, begin by replacing them permanently with God's thoughts about you. Start identifying yourself with God and with what His Word speaks over you. Then you will develop a beautiful mind and start seeing the blessings and the promises of God come to pass in your life.

God loves to change people's identities so they can line up with their destinies. In the scriptures, we see God changed Jacob's identity to line up with His plan for Jacob's destiny. As a grandson of Abraham, he was pivotal in fulfilling the promise God made to Abraham. His old name, Jacob, meant

Supplanter and stood for "to supersede (another) especially by force or treachery" (Merriam-Wester.com).

God had to change his name to line up with his heritage and destiny. Jacob wrestled with an angel of God one night and asked the angel to bless him. The angel asked him, *"What is your name?" "Jacob," he answered. Then the angel said, "Your name will no longer be Jacob, but Israel because you have struggled with God and with humans and have overcome"* (Genesis 32:27-28, NIV).

The angel of God changed Jacob's identity that night. From that time on, his posterity has been called the children of Israel to this day. In the same manner, God has also changed your identity to line up with His plan and His will for your life. The Scripture says, *"Fear not, for I have redeemed you; I have called you by your name; You are Mine" (Isaiah 43:1, NKJV).* God calls you His own and calls you by your name in Christ. You are the redeemed one and the redeemed of the Lord should say so (Psalm 107:2).

The real you (the redeemed one of Christ) is right now perfect, healed, blessed, saved, and righteous. Your new nature does not dwell in anger or quickly gets upset, does not get discouraged or anxious, does not get depressed, is not worried, and does not give up. The real you has a beautiful mind and is exactly like God.

Remember that you are right now an heir of God and a joint heir with Christ. The Scripture says you are just like Jesus in this world (1 John 4:17); therefore, your identity is in Christ and you are complete in Him. Please, affirm the scriptures below to yourself, meditate on them to renew your mind about your new identity in Christ.

AFFIRMATIONS OF IDENTITY IN CHRIST

I have been raised to life with Christ, so I set my heart on things that are in heaven, where Christ sits on His throne at the right hand of God

— COLOSSIANS 3: 1

God made Him who had no sin to be sin for me so that in Him I may become the righteousness of God in Christ

— 2 CORINTHIANS 5:21

Since I am His child, then I am an heir— an heir of God and co-heirs with Christ

—ROMANS 8:17

I am born of God, and I overcome the world, and the victory that has overcome the world is my faith

— 1 JOHN 5:4

As Jesus is, so am I also in this world

— 1 JOHN 4:17

My real life is Christ, and when He appears, I too will appear with him and share His glory!

— COLOSSIANS 3:4

I am perfect, just like my heavenly Father is perfect

— MATTHEW 5:48

I keep my mind fixed on things above, not on things here on earth

— COLOSSIANS 3: 2

I am in Christ, and I am a new creation, a new person on the inside. The former things have passed away. Everything is now new

— 2 CORINTHIANS 5:17

This is what the LORD says, who created me and formed me, "Fear not, for I have redeemed you; I have called you by your name; You are Mine

— ISAIAH 43:1

I know that the LORD He is God: it is Him that made me. I did not make myself; I am His child and the sheep of His pasture

— PSALM 100:3

For I have died, and my life is hidden with Christ in God

— COLOSSIANS 3:3

A WORD FILLED MIND

"Learn to think in line with God's Word."

— KENNETH E. HAGIN

Scripture Reading:

"Thy word have I hid in mine heart, that I might not sin against thee"

— PSALM 119:11, KJV

The Word Of God

God's Word is essential in the life of a believer in Christ. The Word of God is life, gives us light, produces healing, wholeness and guides us if we choose to live according to its instructions. God speaks to us through His Words, and His Words reveal what God thinks about us. It reveals His character and what He plans to do.

The Word of God reveals the will of God for our lives. The only way to find out if we live according to God's will in our daily lives is to know what God says about it. God's Word is for our guidance, instruction, and correction. The Scripture says, *"All Scripture is inspired by God and is useful to teach us what is true and to make us realize what is wrong in our lives. It corrects us when we are wrong and teaches us to do what is right"* (2 Timothy 3:16, NLT).

God sent us His Word through Jesus, His Son, and the Word of God has existed from the very beginning in the form of Jesus. The Scripture says, *"In the beginning was the Word and the Word was with God, and the Word was God"* (John 1:1, NKJV).

Jesus is the Word that has existed from the beginning of time and through whom God made all things (John 1: 3), including mankind. So, we are all a product of God's Word, and everything, us included, is sustained by the Word of God (Hebrews 1:3).

Jesus is the Word of God because He reveals what God is like to us. He is the Word of God that became flesh so He can live among us. Jesus told us in Matthew 4:4 that we are not to live by bread alone, but we are to order our lives by every Word that God speaks. Mankind was created to live and be sustained by the Word of God because His Word is life.

How God's Word Works

The Word of God can help rewire your mind and the way you think until you develop a beautiful mind and your entire mindset is changed. It will inspire you and give you the strength and wisdom you need to make your walk count for Jesus Christ. The power inherent in the Word of God can produce life and change your heart from the inside. The Scripture says, *"For the Word of God is alive and powerful. It is sharper than the sharpest two-edged sword, cutting between soul and spirit, between joint and marrow. It exposes our innermost thoughts and desires"* (Hebrews 4:12, NLT).

In His parable of the sower, Jesus likens God's Word to a seed sown in the soil. He compared different kinds of soils to the condition of our hearts. How well God's Word grows depends on what type of soil (heart) the seed is sown. According to Jesus, the best kind of heart is the one that hears the Word of God, understands it, and does it. That heart will produce an abundant harvest (Matthew 13:1-20).

The only way our hearts can be prepared as a good ground for God's Word is to set our hearts on meditating His Word constantly. The psalmist said that the only way to cleanse our ways was by taking heed to the Word of God (Psalm 119:9). God's command to Joshua was to meditate on His Word all the time so that he would prosper and enjoy good success in everything he did (Joshua 1:8).

Many people are resorting to weird meditation practices nowadays, but God asks us to meditate on His Word only, nothing else. Meditation means "engage in contemplation or reflection, to focus one's thoughts, to reflect and ponder" (Merriam-Webster's Dictionary). It also means to mutter, to speak, to muse. We are to contemplate, reflect and mutter God's Words to ourselves frequently, muse over it often, and declare it with power from within over every contrary situation in our lives.

The Word Is A Weapon

God's Word is the only weapon that we need to combat negative mindsets, toxic and limiting thoughts. The Scripture says God's Word is like a sword (Hebrews 4:12, Ephesians 6:17). We use it to cut down the enemy of our souls, who is responsible for throwing negative thoughts at us like arrows.

The Word of God is one of the spiritual weapons at our disposal to use against the enemy in our spiritual battles. And yes, we are fighting a war! So, God's Word is a special kind of spiritual weapon. We engage it by hearing, reading, meditating on it, and speaking it out of our mouths. If we persist in it, we will defeat the thoughts and the problems we are facing. Therefore, persistence is one of the keys to beating the enemy.

Even Jesus had to do this. When He started His public ministry, He had just finished a forty-day fast, when the devil came to tempt Him. The Bible records that Jesus replied to the devil by quoting God's Word saying, "It is written." The devil came up with more temptations, but He negated each one with the Word of God and the devil left Him finally for another opportune time (Matthew 4:1-11). If Jesus had to use the Word of God to defeat the devil, we too must take His example and defeat the enemy with God's Word.

We should not merely listen to the Word, but we must do the Word if we want to get results and walk in victory. If we're going to overcome worry, anxiety, and negative thoughts and always think like Jesus, we need to apply the weapon of God's Word to our minds. The Scriptures clearly state in James 1:22 that we deceive ourselves if we hear the Word and do not do what it says.

Meditate On The Word

To be able to do what God's Word says, it must become a part of us. We have to read it, hear it, and meditate on it. God told Joshua to meditate on His Word day and night. Everyone can engage in the practice of meditation as God invites us to. Let me repeat: Everyone can do this! Most of us know how to fret and worry, which is a negative form of meditation.

When we are worried, we start to mull a situation and a negative outcome over and over in our minds until it causes us to be depressed, anxious, angry, and so on. Instead, everyone can take God's Word and meditate on it. It yields positive results to do so! God's Word will illuminate our minds as the Word of God has the power to bring light, relief, joy, and success into our situation. Like a revelation we did not have before, we will come to realize that God is our helper.

To start the meditation process, identify the areas in your life that are being attacked by the enemy of your soul and then, find out what God's Word says about those areas. For example, if you are bombarded with thoughts of loneliness, that no one loves you, take the Word of God to fight those thoughts. Declare what God has said. Say something like, "God promised that He is always with me and will never leave nor forsake me. He is with me now. He is for me, with me, and in me, Jesus died for me, He loves me, and I am his child", ... so you get the picture.

Keep on mulling over this truth by muttering it to yourself. As you do this, you will defeat those thoughts and tear down their grip or stronghold over you. Meditating on God's Word will fill you with God's love and warmth, and you will walk in victory in this area. You can then use this method to find freedom, peace, and eventually victory in every other aspect that you need your mind renewed. Now it is time to rehearse scriptures that will help you fill your mind with God's Word and develop a beautiful mind in you.

AFFIRMATIONS TO PRODUCE A WORD-FILLED MIND

I do not live on bread alone, but I live by every Word that comes from the mouth of God

— MATTHEW 4:4

Faith comes to me by hearing and hearing by the Word of God

— ROMANS 10:17

I choose to get rid of all the filth and evil in my life, and I humbly accept the Word God has planted in my heart, for it has the power to save my soul

— JAMES 1:21

God sent His Word to me, healed me, and delivered me from my destructions

— PSALM 107:20

Lord, I have hidden Your word in my heart, that I might not sin against You

— PSALM 119:11

I present myself to God approved, a worker who does not need to be ashamed and who correctly handles the Word of truth

— 2 TIMOTHY 2:15

I let the message of Christ dwell in me richly

— COLOSSIANS 3:16

I wear the helmet of salvation and the sword of the Spirit, which is the Word of God

— EPHESIANS 6:17

God's words do not return to me empty, but it accomplishes what I desire and achieves the purpose for which I sent it

— ISAIAH 55:11

I am blessed because I hear the Word of God and obey it.

— LUKE 11:28

It is the Spirit who gives me life; the flesh profits nothing. The words that Jesus speaks to me are Spirit, and they are life

— JOHN 6:63

Your Word is a lamp unto my feet and a light unto my path

— PSALM 119:105

May the words I speak and the meditation of my heart be pleasing to you, my Rock, my Lord, and my Redeemer

— PSALM 19:14

I am already clean because of the Word Jesus has spoken to me

— JOHN 15:3

Lord, order my footsteps according to Your Word

— PSALM 119:133

3

BIG DREAMS AND VISIONS

"If you can't be a sun, be a star. For it isn't by size that you win or fail. Be the best of whatever you are."

— MARTIN LUTHER KING JR.

Scripture Reading:

"The Lord said to Abram after Lot had parted from him, Look around from where you are, to the north and south, to the east and west. All the land that you see I will give to you and your offspring forever. I will make your offspring like the dust of the earth so that if anyone could count the

dust, then your offspring could be counted. Go, walk through the length and breadth of the land, for I am giving it to you"
— GENESIS 13: 14-17, NIV

Dare To Dream

The dictionary defines vision as the "faculty or state of being able to see"; "the ability to think about or plan the future with imagination or wisdom, something that you imagine: a picture that you see in your mind" (Oxford English Dictionary). God has given us the ability to dream (see with our inner eyes), and He wants us to dream big, so He can help us fulfill them. He said He would fill our mouths with good things if we open them wide (Psalm 81:10).

We all have dreams and visions for our lives that we, as believers, want to see accomplished. Such dreams, goals, or visions obviously must align with God's plan for our lives. A valid question to ask is, "How do I know if my dreams are in line with God's plan, especially those dreams and goals that are not explicitly spelled out in the Bible?" Let me explain: As a born-again believer, the Spirit of God dwells in you, and you are one Spirit with God. This means that God's Spirit in you deposits ideas, desires, dreams, and goals in your heart. How can you judge if these ideas are actually coming from God? By using God's Word. For example, are your dreams and desires pure, holy, virtuous, and praiseworthy? Are they a blessing to you and others, or are they harmful and a threat to your spiritual growth, as well as others? Depending on what answers you get to these questions, you can ascertain whether your ideas and desires are from God or not.

God loves you, and He is a good Father, so even if you missed His voice and you make a wrong decision or went in the wrong direction, it is OK. As soon as you realize it, you acknowledge that you missed it, learn from your mistakes, move on and get back to doing what God has put in your heart to do. I know that God put those dreams, desires, goals, and visions in your heart because He loves you. He ultimately believes in your ability to fulfill them, and indeed, in one way or the other, He will help you achieve them if you let Him.

There are two kinds of visions: Natural vision, which is, seeing with your natural eyes, and believing because you have seen. The second type of vision is Spiritual vision which is when you see with your inner eyes of faith, even though there is no physical evidence to substantiate what you see. This chapter will focus on the spiritual vision aspect as everyone uses spiritual vision either positively or negatively.

Seeing With Your Inner Eyes

Your mind can see. God made it so. For example, if I say elephant, what do you see? A chicken, a dog? No. The word 'elephant' produced a vision in your mind. You are seeing with your inner eye when you dream of having, or doing something. The Scripture says that people cast off restraint if there is no vision to keep them in check (Proverbs 29:18). Restraint means a "measure or condition that keeps someone or something under control or within limits" (Lexico.com).

When there is no proper vision, it's easy to lose control or focus. Christians with no vision or direction are like athletes running aimlessly, without a goal or endpoint. Apostle Paul says it is like someone beating the air (1 Corinthians 9:26). A God-given vision also requires focus to keep it in place. Jesus said that your eye must be single for your whole body to be full of light (Mathew 6:22).

God's Words contain God's vision for our lives. God's vision for us is birth into our hearts by hearing and meditating on the Word. Then this vision (mental images created from God's Word) in our hearts helps us focus on what God wants to accomplish in our lives or, in the lives of others through us.

The wonderful thing is that taking the vision or the mental image or picture we receive from God's Word and making it our own produces faith to manifest the vision. So, you can stand on God's promise regarding whatever you desire, and you will see the manifestation of your vision. When you take God's promises to heart and start seeing yourself as God sees you, you become what you see.

Let me bring your attention to a dichotomy we face in life as Christians. When we read the Bible or hear a great sermon or message, we are greatly encouraged, and we feel like we can conquer the world and face anything life brings our way. Then everyday life happens, stuff comes up, and we face the same situations we were dealing with before that we have not yet overcome. This causes us to ponder our failures and problems, and we re-focus on those things as we did before. Due to the dichotomy of what we believe to be true and yet being unable to walk in it, we may become discouraged. In that case, those things, the stuff of life, become magnified in our minds, overcome our faith, and they therefore remain and do not change because they are now our focus and vision.

Each time we ponder over our problems and magnify them in our minds, we are allowing the picture of the promises of God to be replaced by worrisome, negative, self-defeating thoughts of failure and doom. Thus, our faith in God is overcome by thoughts of self-doubt, and we become victim-minded instead of victory-minded.

Change What You See

So, if you want to change your present circumstances, stop looking at them and thinking about them. If you constantly see the same thing on the inside as you see with your natural vision, no change will be produced. You must see a different image of your circumstances. This new image or picture can only be created from God's Word. This is the only way for permanent change to occur.

God does not see as we see. The natural man looks at things the way they are and believes what he sees, but the spiritual man must see things the way God sees them. We must see with our spiritual eyes the vision of the Almighty through His spoken Word. For example, Abraham saw himself as a childless, one-hundred-year-old man. His wife, Sarah, at ninety years old, was doubly dead in her womb (Genesis 17:17). But God saw him differently and talked to him as if he were already the father of many nations. The *Scripture says, "I have made you a father of many nations, in the presence of Him whom he believed,*

God, who gives life to the dead and calls those things which do not exist as though they did" (Romans 4:17, NKJV).

God brings the future into the now and talks about it as if it is already here, and so should we. Abraham had to learn to see as God saw him for any change to happen in his circumstance (Romans 4: 18-20). We should learn to see our circumstances through His eyes as well. Right now, you may be going through a trial in your marriage. You may be undergoing difficulties or challenges at work; maybe you are experiencing financial problems, dealing with rebellious children, or dealing with failing health and a bunch of other issues.

The bigger issue here is that these situations may begin to define your vision because that is what you are constantly seeing. But God, your God, sees a *different image* about you. He sees your marriage blessed, sees you successful at work, sees you supernaturally provided for, and all your needs supplied. He sees your children blessed and taught of the Lord and sees you with a healed and healthy body.

God does not see as a man sees. God looks at the heart while a man looks at the outward appearance (1 Samuel 16:17). God looks at the perfect born again you, and He sees victory. He tells you that you are blessed already with every spiritual blessing in the heavenly places in Christ (Ephesians 1:3).

Speak Your Vision

It is evident from what I have previously said that God, unlike us, does not speak about things as they currently are. Instead, He talks about what is possible and calls the things that do not exist as though they do exist. This is a spiritual principle. Just like God, you, too, are a spirit capable of speaking what you desire into existence. However, if you only acknowledge what you see with your natural eyes and talk about your situation's impossibility, your condition will not change. It will continue to be the same.

On the other hand, if you envision a bright future for yourself, believe it, and speak it out, your reality will change accordingly. In other words, whatever you are saying about yourself, whether positive or negative, will be your reality. So there is no point in stating the obvious. It is not going to change anything. God has given you the power and authority to declare the truth over your life. What God said about your current situation is what is true. God tells you to call those things which do not exist as though they did, and they will exist!

Real change comes when you agree with God's Word and begin to see the result, which is the answer to your problems.

When God asked Abraham to look up from where he was to all the four directions of the new land he would inherit, God was expanding Abraham's vision to see all that God has provided for him. God requires that we be able to see all that He wants to give us before we can make them our reality. Abraham inherited the land, for God told Abraham that all the land as far as he could see was his to possess and enjoy (Genesis 13: 14-15).

God is the same yesterday, today, and forever. You, too, can have ,and make yours, everything your heart can see and your mind can receive, for this is the precursor to receiving the blessings that God wants to give you. Therefore, choose to see the vision of the Almighty. It is always a good vision. Whenever you see your situation through God's eyes, you will find that all your issues will start getting resolved because when you see as He sees, you will be changed into what you see.

God's thoughts are higher than ours. They are thoughts of good, not evil, thoughts that give us hope and a future. God's thoughts release visions of good, blessings, healings, provision, protection, and so on in our hearts. Therefore, start to focus on your God-given dreams and thoughts today so that you can develop a beautiful mind and begin to see the manifestation of your heart's desires. Please, affirm these scriptures to help you build up your mind to attain big dreams and visions for your life.

AFFIRMATIONS FOR DREAMS AND VISIONS

God has great plans for me. They are plans to prosper me and give me hope and a future

— JEREMIAH 29:11

No eye has ever seen, no ear has ever heard, and no mind can imagine what God has prepared for me because I love him

— 1 CORINTHIANS 2:9

I am His child, and He shows me His secret for my life. I do not look at the troubles I can see now; instead, I fix my gaze on unseen things. For the things I see now will soon be gone, but the things I cannot see will last forever

— 2 CORINTHIANS 4:18

Then the Lord answered me: "Write the vision; make it plain on tablets, so he may run who reads it

— HABAKKUK 2:2

The Lord will show me the path of life I need to take

— PSALM 16:11

O *Sovereign LORD! You made the earth and the heavens by your strong hand and mighty arm. Nothing is too hard for you*

— JEREMIAH 32:17

For with God, nothing will be impossible

— LUKE 1:37

All things are possible to me because I believe

— MARK 9:23

I open my mouth wide, and God fills it

—PSALM 81:10

4

OVERCOMING THOUGHT BATTLES

I DECLARE; my thoughts are guided by God's Word every day

— JOEL OSTEEN

Scripture Reading:

"That is why I tell you not to worry about everyday life—whether you have enough food and drink or enough clothes to wear. Isn't life more than food and your body more than clothing? Look at the birds. They do not plant or harvest or store food in barns, for your heavenly Father feeds

them. And aren't you far more valuable to him than they are? Can all your worries add a single moment to your life?"

— MATTHEW 6: 25-33 , NLT

The War Of The Mind Rages On

The current world situation is causing many to become worried, fearful, anxious, and depressed. The enemy of our souls uses every opportunity to attack us daily with thoughts of guilt, condemnation, insufficiency, regret, worry, and fear. There may be conditions and situations in your own life right now that are causing you to be anxious and fearful due to the uncertainty of the outcome of the problem you are facing.

We need to realize that our minds are naturally attracted to finding solutions to our problems. Thus, we tend to be preoccupied with trying to think of solutions to fix the conditions and situations around us that we do not like. We tend to think about solutions from anywhere else, except God's Word.

This preoccupation with thinking of solutions to our problems can consume us entirely. It can drain us of vital energy and strength to meditate on God's Word, as we already discussed in the chapter 'A Word-filled mind.'

I used to be perplexed at my inability to focus on God's thoughts even after just reading my Bible or listening to a beautiful sermon. Instead, I find myself thinking negative, sorry thoughts about the issues I was facing. This happens to us because we are naturally programmed to think negatively! Our mind is drawn to negativity, and this is why it is so much easier to think negative thoughts, but we have to fight our minds to accept and think God's thoughts.

So whenever I find myself distracted during times of reading my Bible and at times of prayer and devotion, or sometimes even during a church service, I realize that it is the work of the enemy. This is how he attacks us and spins our minds into doubt, worry, and unbelief over what God has spoken to prevent us from receiving our victory. He knows that thoughts are important and that what we think persistently is what we become. The word of God says as a man thinks, so is he (Proverbs 23:7).

God's Thoughts

There are high thoughts and low thoughts. Low thoughts are those that sink our souls into darkness, anger, despair, discouragement, depression, resentment, and bitterness. On the other hand, high thoughts are those that line up with God's promises for us. As we think of them, they often improve our mood, encourage us, build us up on the inside, provide light, clarity, and solutions to problems and build faith in our hearts.

God invites us to take His thoughts because they are high thoughts. God's thoughts are those thoughts that line up with God's Word. The spirit of God dwells in us, and when we are in tune with the Holy Spirit and are led by Him, God's thoughts dominate our being.

As sons and daughters of God, we should follow God's direction. He said we should not be anxious about anything but cast all our cares upon Him (1 Peter 5:7). Casting our cares upon Him means leaving everything in His hands and resting totally in Him. We choose to step back from being careful and concerned. Instead, we surrender our entire being with all our burdens, cares, and worries at the feet of Jesus.

Our response to the circumstances, conditions, fear, anxiety and negative thinking that comes up in our lives is to remember that we have been called to enter into rest as God's people. Then we are encouraged to labor to remain at rest, remembering that God is our peace, protection, source and that He has not given us the spirit of fear (Hebrews 4: 9-11).

Resting in God's Word means declaring the answer over the situation. The answer is what God's Word promised you for your situation. When you find the solution in the Word of God, then stay there (rest there), diligently and persistently, until the desired result manifests, for, with faith and patience, we inherit the promise (Hebrews 6:12).

Your circumstances may be causing you a lot of stress and anxiety right now and taking your peace away. God knows exactly what your needs are. He invites you to come before him and cast all those cares upon Him. We are not to be anxious about anything but pray about everything (Philippians 4:6).

Beautify Your Mind God's Way

To eliminate negative thinking and develop a genuinely lasting positive mindset, we need to follow God's instructions. The Scripture says, *"For my thoughts are not your thoughts, neither are your ways my ways," declares the LORD. "As the heavens are higher than the earth, so are my ways higher than your ways and my thoughts than your thoughts "* (Isaiah 55:8-9, NIV).

To develop a lasting positive mindset, do not pay attention to, or meditate on, the things that are troubling you now. If you give your attention to them as you always did, those conditions will remain and not change. That is the natural way, the way everyone else does it. We are to do it God's way, which is not to consider our problems. We are told not to copy the behavior and customs of this world. Instead, we should allow God to transform us into totally new persons by changing the way we think about things (Romans 12:2).

The conditions and the circumstances you are facing right now will pressure you to accept things the way they are because it is so much easier to go with the flow. When you meditate on, worry about, and are anxious about the issues in your life, you are conforming to the customs and behavior of the old man of the flesh. The danger in this is that as you continue to live by the customs and behaviors of the natural man, the problems in your life will not go away. Instead, they will continue to persist, and nothing will change.

If you want to truly change your circumstances, you need a transformed mind. You need to think differently. Start by meditating and remembering what Jesus did on the cross and the victory that is already yours in Christ. Remember and keep remembering! Purposefully allow God's Word to dominate your mind. The Scripture says you should let the Word of God dwell richly in you (Colossians 3:16). You may have to do this repeatedly for a while before your mind gets the picture that change is needed. As your mind begins to line up with God's word, it will start to produce different images. These are often images of courage, confidence, victory, I can do all things mindset, and all things are possible, mindset. These God-given images or pictures produced from God's Word are the fundamental catalysts for change.

Instead, if you spend your time focusing on, thinking about, remembering, and seeing only the things that are stressing you out; the unfavorable circumstances, sickness, bad economy, and everything else that is going on, what happens then? In that case, you will continue to get those things that you focus on because it is a spiritual principle. That is why God wants you to remember His Word and His promises to you about your situation. Then receive them into your heart and meditate on them to produce His vision of good in you so that you can experience His goodness.

Scripture says that Jesus already destroyed those things in your life that are stressing you out right now and causing destruction, anxiety, and pain in your life (1 John 3:8b). They are thieves meant to steal your joy, faith, and peace. But Jesus has come to deliver you and give you life in its fullness (John 10: 10).

God's plan for sending Jesus is for His people to experience and enjoy life in abundance. If you believe, receive, and meditate on this, you will experience freedom from destructive thoughts and win your thought battles. Now, keep the following scriptures in front of your eyes so that, as you meditate and speak them, you will become a strong warrior, winning your thought battles daily, and you will develop a beautiful mind.

AFFIRMATIONS TO OVERCOME THOUGHT BATTLES

I lay all my cares and anxiety on Him because He cares for me

— 1 PETER 5:7

I choose to think about what is true, honorable things, pure things, whatever is lovely, whatever is commendable, things that are excellent, and things worthy of praise, as God commands

— PHILIPPIANS 4:8

I have not been given a spirit of fear but of power, love, and a sound mind
— 2 TIMOTHY 1:7

I am kept in amazingly perfect peace because I trust in God, and my thoughts and my mind are fixed on Him

— ISAIAH 26:3

Though I walk in the flesh, I do not wage war after the flesh. I cast down every imagination, argument, and every high and lofty thing that exalts itself against the knowledge of God. I now take every thought captive and bring them under the Lordship of Jesus

— 2 CORINTHIANS 10:3-5

I rejoice in the Lord always. I choose not to stress about anything but instead to pray about everything. With a thankful heart, I let my prayer requests be made known to God. And I let the peace of God, which surpasses all understanding, guard my heart and my mind in Christ Jesus

— PHILIPPIANS 4:4-9

I have been raised with Christ, so I set my heart on heavenly things, where Christ is sitting at the right hand of God

— COLOSSIANS 3:1

Above all else, I guard my heart, for everything I do flows from it. It determines how I live my life

— PROVERBS 4:23

God's thoughts are higher than mine. They are thoughts of good, not evil, thoughts that give me hope and a future

— JEREMIAH 29:11

I call unto the Lord, and He answers me and shows me great things that I did not know before

— JEREMIAH 33:3

I choose not to conform myself to this world but to be transformed by the renewal of my mind, that I may be able to discern the will of God and what is good, perfect, and acceptable

— ROMANS 12:2

5

A WELL AND HEALED BODY

"Jesus Christ accomplished everything that God the Father started at the creation, and that includes total health."

— ROD PARSLEY

Scripture Reading:

"Surely, He has borne our griefs and carried carried our sorrows; Yet we esteemed Him stricken, smitten by God, and afflicted. But He was wounded for our transgressions; He was bruised for our

iniquities; The chastisement for our peace was upon Him, And by His stripes, we are healed"

— ISAIAH 53: 4-5, KJV

Healing Is God's Will

In this chapter, we will discuss how healing and wholeness are God's will for us so that you can build up your faith in this area to fight the lies of the enemy of your soul. Matthew 4:23 says Jesus preached the good news and healed all kinds of sickness and disease. Acts 10:38 says Jesus went about doing good and healing all those who the devil had afflicted with illnesses and other health conditions. So we see Jesus Himself prove that God wants us to be in health and wholeness.

We read the story of the man with leprosy who came to Jesus to be healed of his disease. He came, but he was unsure of Jesus' willingness to make him well. He had heard about how Jesus was healing everyone, so he did not question Jesus' ability to heal, but he was just not sure if Jesus was willing to heal him (Matthew 8:1).

Many sons and daughters of God suffer from all kinds of incurable ailments today, but just like that man with leprosy, they do not know if Jesus is willing to heal them. Some have placed their trust in the doctor's word and taken it as gospel because the doctor told them there was no hope for their conditions. They still believe in God's ability to heal them if He wants to, but they are unsure of His willingness to do so. Some have completely misunderstood God's desire to set people free from sickness. They believe their sickness is God's way of disciplining them. Some even go as far as saying that their sickness and diseases are God's cross for them to bear and that they are suffering for Jesus.

Such a mindset does not align with who God is or why He sent Jesus to come and redeem us. Jesus healed sick people in His day. The Scripture says that the Son of God was made manifest to destroy the devil's works (1 John 3:8). The very purpose He came was to destroy everything that the devil did at the fall of man in the garden of Eden. The God who created our bodies is also the healer of our bodies. Psalm 107:20 says that God sends His Word to heal those that are being destroyed by sicknesses. Sickness and disease are not of God. It is the work of the devil.

So, to the man with leprosy, Jesus answered, *"I am willing, be cleansed"* (Matthew 8: 2-3, NKJV). This answer is for everyone, no matter what ailment you are suffering from. Jesus is not only able, but He is willing to heal you and has already gone to the cross and died to pay the price for you to be well. Therefore, health and wholeness are very much a part of God's plan for your life. The Scripture says, *"This was to fulfill what was spoken through the prophet Isaiah: "He took up our infirmities and bore our diseases"* (Matthew 8:17, NKJV).

Jesus Took Our Sicknesses

Jesus took your infirmities, anxieties and sicknesses, and diseases. This then implies that you no longer have them because Jesus took them. They do not belong to you anymore. Yes, illness and disease may be currently ravaging your body in the natural. That is not to be denied. But remember that you are in a spiritual battle for your life. The scriptures say that even though we walk in the flesh, we do not war after the flesh, using natural weapons (2 Corinthians 10:3). The weapon we use in this spiritual warfare for our health and healing is the Word of God.

The concept of looking to Jesus as our redeeming sacrifice was first introduced in the book of Numbers. The people of Israel had sinned against God, so, He sent serpents to invade their camp, and the snakes started biting them as punishment for their sins, so much so that they died by the thousands. They began to cry unto Moses, who, in turn, cried out to God on their behalf. God directed Moses to make a bronze serpent and lift it up on a pole and ask the people of Israel whom snakes had bitten to look at the pole, and they would be healed. The Scripture says, *"Just as Moses lifted up the snake in the wilderness, so the Son of Man must be lifted up"* (John 3:14, NIV).

Just as Moses lifted the bronze serpent on the pole in the desert, in the same way, Jesus was lifted up on the cross for our salvation. When we look to Jesus' death on the cross, our sins are forgiven. Our sicknesses and diseases are healed because Jesus paid the price on the cross for everything, including all illnesses, diseases, and disorders, once and for all.

How To Receive Healing

To appropriate your healing, you must persist in a state of mind that sees yourself as healed because Jesus took your sickness. Do you believe in the Word of God? How could Jesus have taken your sicknesses and diseases, and you still have them? It's impossible. You must be in faith and receive your healing through the finished work of the cross. You can only have faith when you consciously agree with the Word of God by renewing your mind to the fact that Jesus took your place. Be continuously aware of God's life within you. His life in you is what sustains your body. When your mind tells you that you can't get well, *refuse* to accept it. If what your mind tells you disagrees with God's Word, do not believe it. Renew your mind with the Word of God and His promises regarding your healing. Keep meditating on His Word until your mind can accept that you are already healed and delivered from the condition in your body. Do this until your mind can accept that you have the very blessing that you desire already. You will be unable to receive healing until your mind agrees with and *wholeheartedly* accepts the truth of God's Word.

Child of God, please know that your mind will fight you throughout this process. Your mind will constantly draw your attention to what you see happening in your body. This is where the spiritual fight comes in. This is where you begin to cast down and negate any thoughts outside the promise of healing and health for you (2 Corinthians 10:5).

However, as you continue to keep God's Word before your eyes, you will eventually enter into a state of rest in the finished work of the cross. Your heart will completely agree with God's Word, and then your healing will manifest. Approach every problem in life as a spiritual one with the mentality that I am already victorious through what Jesus has done (1 Corinthians 15:57).

In the story told in Mark 9: 14-26, the boy's father came to Jesus and asked if there was anything Jesus could do to heal his boy. He was desperate and could not see how his boy could be healed. He wanted Jesus to heal him. The Scripture says, *"Jesus said to him, "If you can believe, all things are possible to him who believes"* (Mark 9:23, NKJV).

From the way the man entrusted the boy's healing entirely to Jesus, I get the feeling that he left it all to Jesus to take complete control. What is wrong with that, you ask? Well, Jesus's answer clarifies it for us. Jesus said, "Oh no, you too have a part to play—you have to *believe*, for it is by *your* believing that your boy will be healed." In other words, He was saying, "Do not put this on me" (my paraphrase). By asking the boy's father to believe, Jesus laid the responsibility and the power to control the outcome back on him and said that the boy could only be healed if the father could believe (see with his eye of faith that it was possible).

Most of us Christians are like that boy's father today. We are waiting for God to do something about our healing. It is like the man the Bible described at the pool of Bethesda, who was waiting for thirty-eight years to get into the healing pool (John 5:1-8). When Jesus asked if he wanted to be healed, he had a list of excuses why he was not yet healed. Jesus did not ask for his reasons but whether he wanted to be healed because it is available now. So God has already done everything about our healing. The ball is now in our court. We have to receive by faith.

As we discussed already, you need to be in faith to receive your healing through the finished work of the cross. It is available to you now, anytime and anywhere you are. You don't have to attend a prayer meeting, an adoration service, or have a famous healing evangelist lay hands on you. God has already healed you, and you can receive your healing at *any time*. The moment you have faith for healing, you will be healed. Faith for healing comes by hearing God's Words. Healing is available to you NOW! Can you see it? No, do not look at what is happening in your body! That is natural sight. Look inside, in your spirit-man. Can you see it? Not yet? OK, go back to your healing scriptures.

Faith for healing comes by hearing what God has promised about healing and wholeness. Read those scriptures and continue to meditate on them. The Scripture says, "*My son pay attention to what I say, turn your ear to my Words. Do not let them out of your sight, keep them within your heart; for they are life to those who find them and health to one's whole body*" (Proverbs 4:22, NIV).

Mull the healing scriptures over and over. Say them out loud. Sing them. Personalize them. Visualize them. Now can you see? Good, because what you see is what is possible for you. Think about that! Jesus said If you can believe! The outcome of the situation depends entirely on you. It is under your control because He has already done His part to remove every legal right the enemy had to inflict sickness on you. He already became sick with your disease so that you can be well. If you can see it happening, you will receive it.

I have packed a punch of Scripture in this chapter to show you that sickness or disease does not have any power to stay any longer in your body. Confess them always to develop a beautiful mind free of worry, anxiety, and negative thoughts so that you can receive the gift of healing and wholeness that Jesus has given to you.

AFFIRMATIONS FOR A WELL AND HEALED BODY

My soul praises You, LORD, and I forget not all Your benefits -You forgives all my sins and heals all my diseases. You save my life from the pit and crowns me with love and compassion

— PSALM 103:2-4

My faith has healed me and makes me whole. I go in peace, and I am freed from my suffering

— MARK 5:34

It was spoken through the prophet Isaiah:Jesus took up my infirmities and bore my diseases

— MATTHEW 8:17

I serve the LORD, my God, for He has blessed my food and my water. And He has taken sickness and diseases away from me

— EXODUS 23:25

He sent His Word and healed me and delivered me from my destructions

— PSALM 107:20

God infuses me with strength when I am weary and increases my power when I am weak.

— ISAIAH 40:29

I hope in the Lord, and he renews my strength. I will soar on wings like eagles; I will run and not grow weary. I will walk, and I will not faint

— ISAIAH 40:31

I attend to what God says; I turn my ears to His words. I do not let them out of my sight; I keep them within my heart, for they are life to me because I found them, and they are health to my whole body

— PROVERBS 4: 20-22

God restores me to health and heals my wounds

— JEREMIAH 30:17

He bore my sins in His body on the tree that I might die to sin and live to righteousness. By His stripes, I have been healed

— 1 PETER 2:24

God heals me when I am brokenhearted and binds up my wounds

— PSALM 147:3

My heart and my flesh may fail, but God is the strength of my heart and my portion forever

— PSALM 73:26, NIV

Heal me, O LORD, and I shall be healed; save me, and I shall be saved, for you are my praise

— JEREMIAH 17:14, NIV

6

THE TABLE IS PREPARED

"This world is full of opportunities, but it will ONLY take you the Favor of God to get one."

— DOUGLAS YAW MENSAH

Scripture Reading:

"You prepare a table before me in the presence of my enemies. You anoint my head with oil; my cup overflows"

— PSALM 23:5, NIV

A Bountiful Table

God has already prepared and blessed us with every spiritual blessing. God is a God of abundance, all-sufficiency and everything in the world belongs to Him. He has prepared a table of blessings for us. Everything we will ever need is on the table. He promised He would supply all our needs and bless us according to His riches in glory. Through Jesus, we have everything we need.

Many Christians know and often declare that they are blessed. For many, that is where it ends. They are not really experiencing the blessing in their lives. Some are still living under the hold of the curse of the law. The Scripture says that we are already redeemed from every curse (Galatians 3:13). Jesus redeemed us from the curse so that we can walk in the blessing of Abraham.

The blessing is like a prepared table. This table has everything we could ever need. We can approach the table and take what we need to overcome every situation in life. The table is always accessible by faith through Jesus Christ. We have been given all that pertains to life and godliness (2 Peter 1:3).

Many people think that the blessing of the Lord only encompasses physical and material things. The blessing is way more than that. It includes peace of mind, health, the joy of the Lord as well as physical and material things. God has already given us every spiritual blessing as we read in Ephesians 1:3. The blessing is also the *power given by God to experience and enjoy all the things God has given us.*

The Blessing Is Visible

We see God bless Abraham in Genesis 12:2, promising to make him a great nation. He also promised that the whole earth would be blessed through him (Genesis 18:18), and God always keeps His promises. The blessing He promised Abraham comes to us through our inheritance in Christ (as part of the new covenant we have in Christ).

The blessing on someone's life can be seen. The Bible talks about how Potiphar saw the blessing on Joseph, who was a slave in his house. He saw how the blessing on Joseph's life was prospering his household. Even when Joseph ended up in prison due to a false accusation from Potiphar's wife, the blessing and favor of the Lord were still upon him. It set him apart even in prison. Finally, the blessing paved the way for him to become the second most powerful man in Egypt.

King Abimelech and his people saw how much God had prospered Isaac compared to them. Any place Isaac went, the Lord blessed him and caused him to grow and increase in wealth and fortune. Even during the time of famine, when everyone else was starving to death, Isaac prospered. The Scripture says, *"Isaac planted crops in that land and the same year reaped a hundredfold because the LORD blessed him"* (Genesis 26:12, NIV). King Abimelech and his people began to envy Isaac because of how much he prospered, and then they kicked him out of their land. Isaac continued to thrive in all his sojournings.

The blessing could be seen in Jacob's life as well. It caused him to prosper even when Laban, his father-in-law, tried to cheat him. The Scripture says, *"yet your Father has cheated me by changing my wages ten times. However, God has not allowed him to harm me. If he said, 'The speckled ones will be your wages,' then all the flocks gave birth to speckled young; and if he said, 'The streaked ones will be your wages,' then all the flocks bore streaked young. So, God has taken away your Father's livestock and has given them to me"* (Genesis 31:7-9, NIV).

Laban tried to cheat Jacob, who was under the covenant that God had with his grandfather Abraham. In the process of time, Laban lost everything to Jacob.

So dear child of God, when you have the blessing in your life, no one can put you down. You will always rise up and come out on top. But do not be deluded into thinking that God is blessing you because you are the most intelligent or talented person in your workplace, business, or whatever you do. The real reason is that God has favored you and prepared a table for you so that you can testify to His goodness, saying, "It is the Lord who has blessed me, and I couldn't be who I am or have what I have except for Him."

Blessed And Not Cursed

So, the blessing in your life is of and from the Lord. It cannot be taken away. When you are blessed, you cannot be cursed. The enemies of Israel hired Balaam to curse the children of Israel so that they would be defeated in battle. But God met Balaam on the way, intervened, and told Balaam not to curse the people because they were already blessed (Numbers 22:12).

The enemies of Israel were not happy with Balaam because he would not curse Isreal. He was the best prophet in the land and whomever he cursed was toast! So, they kept pressuring Balaam to curse Israel. Balaam replied,"*How shall I curse whom God has not cursed? And how shall I denounce whom the LORD has not denounced?*" (Numbers 23:8, NIV).

The enemy of your soul can try to put obstacles in your way. He may be trying to stop you from advancing in your career, business, ministry, relationships, and other areas of your life, but he will not succeed. Why? Because you are blessed and not cursed. Scripture says any weapon forged against you will not prevail (Isaiah 54:17). You will overcome anything that comes against the plan and will of God for your life because of the blessing that is on you.

The blessing came on us as an inheritance through Jesus Christ. To receive and experience this benefit in your life, you must know it is yours through your covenant relationship and then take it by faith. Believe and begin to see yourself blessed even when you have no natural evidence for it at first. It is yours to receive and walk in and will start to manifest in your life as you stand your ground in faith for the blessing. Our connectedness with God through Jesus causes everything around us to prosper: spiritually, physically, emotionally, financially, and in every other area of our lives.

The Blessing Cannot Be Stopped

The Scripture says, *"The blessing of the LORD makes one rich, and He adds no sorrow with it"* (Proverbs 10:22, NKJV). The blessing will bring the necessary resources to you and draw the right people to you and cause them to help you. God invites us to choose the blessing (Deuteronomy 30:19). Many people unknowingly choose the curse by their actions and the words they speak out of line with God's Word.

God has blessed his people already and has given us the *power* to overcome and do things in our lives that look impossible. The blessing of God in our lives opens doors for good things to come to us. God had prepared a way before us because He is the good Shepherd who leads us into green pastures.

When you walk in the blessing, you know that God is for you. God says I am your shield and your exceeding great reward. God is with you, for you, and He is in you. You are not on your own, and He has blessed you with supernatural blessings that make supernatural things happen.

No one can stop the blessing of God in your life. The only one that can stop it is you. If you are in a state of unbelief, that will prevent you from assessing the blessing. Those around you, that is, the kind of friendships you have or the kind of environments you find yourself in, might hinder the blessing. That is why God asked Abraham to move away from his old place to a new one. Sometimes, you must leave your environment and your friends, job, or even your city to walk in the blessing. *Listen to what the Spirit of God says to do.* All your dreams, goals, and the provisions you need are all supplied and empowered by the blessing. The blessing causes all things to be well.

The affirmation scriptures below will renew and beautify your mind plus revitalize your faith to believe God for His supernatural power to flow into your life, causing your blessings to overflow.

AFFIRMATIONS FOR THE TABLE IS PREPARED

I am convinced that God, who has begun a good work in me, will continue it until it is completed

— PHILIPPIANS 1:6

I refuse to worry about everyday life. God knows my needs and supplies them because I seek His Kingdom and His righteousness

— MATTHEW 6:33

The blessing of the Lord is on me and my house. We are blessed when we go out and blessed when we come in

— DEUTERONOMY 28:6

Whatever job or business that I do, I do it well and with all my might by the grace of God

— ECCLESIASTES 9:10

I am like a tree planted by streams of water. My life bears fruit and prospers because I meditate on God's Word

— PSALM 1:1-2

I obey the command of the Lord. I open my mouth wide, and the Lord will fill it

— PSALM 81:10

My LORD, God is a sun and shield; the LORD bestows favor and honor on me. He does not withhold anything good from me because I walk uprightly

— PSALM 84:11

My God supplies all my needs according to His riches in glory

— PHILIPPIANS 4:19

Jesus came to give me life in abundance

— JOHN 10:10

I can and will do all things through Christ, who gives me strength

— PHILIPPIANS 4: 13

The Lord is my good Shepherd. I have no lack or want of anything. He provides for all my needs

— PSALMS 23:1

Because I seek the Lord with all my heart, I lack no good thing

—PSALMS 34:10

I draw near to the throne of grace with confidence, and there I receive mercy and find grace to help me in time of need

— HEBREWS 4:16

7

A LIFE OF FAITH

"If a tiny virus can do this much damage, imagine what mustard seed-size faith can do. Believe in His mercy."

— RONNIE (RON) MILLEVO

Scripture Reading:

"According as God has dealt to every man the measure of faith"

— ROMANS 12:3, KJV

What Faith Is

God the Father has given all His children a measure of faith, so we all have the same amount or measure of faith. This amount of faith that we have received can be increased or decreased. The Bible says we can increase our faith by hearing God's Word (Romans 10:17). God's Word is food for our faith. When we read God's Word every day and meditate on it all the time, it will help us develop our faith.

Another way the Scripture tells us we can increase our faith is to use it, exercising it by putting it into practice (Hebrews 5:11). This, then, also means that faith goes away or is suppressed when we hear words opposing the Word of God. Hearing Words that produce fear, discouragement, worry, anxiety, and so on will diminish our faith. Also, putting it into practice by acting out of fear will significantly weaken our faith.

What then is faith? Faith is the confident assurance that something we want will happen (we all have things we believe for and want to happen). Faith is the certainty that what we hope for is waiting for us, even though we cannot see it up ahead (Hebrews 11:1). To have faith in God is to believe that He will do what He said He would do. Faith believes the spoken and the written Word of God to be real and accurate, even though we may not be able to verify it with our natural senses.

You hear people say, "I will believe it when I see it," but this is contrary to what the Bible teaches. God is a Spirit and operates in the realm of faith. His method of operation is to believe first and then see. This is a spiritual principle. Jesus said, *"Because you have seen me, you have believed; blessed are those who have not seen and yet have believed"* (John 20:29, NIV).

Faith Is A Spiritual Weapon

Everything in this physical world first existed in the spirit realm before existing in the natural realm (Hebrews 11:2). We live in and are surrounded by the spiritual world where circumstances are controlled by faith or fear. You and I are operating by one of these forces all the time. There is no neutral ground. We are in a spiritual faith battle. This is the reason Apostle Paul encourages us to fight the good fight of faith (1 Timothy 6:12) and fight not as one that beats the air (1 Corinthians 9:26). Fighting the fight of faith means standing your ground to receive what Jesus died and paid for.

Some Christians do not even realize that they are in a spiritual battle. They just go with whatever situation comes into their lives. They feel they have absolutely no control over the issues of life that comes up. Whatever will be will be, they say. But this is so far out of God's system. The Scripture says that the weapons we fight with are not the weapons of the world (2 Corinthians 10:4). God has given us various spiritual weapons to fight our faith battle with and take control of situations that come into our lives with His help.

As Christians, we walk by faith and not by sight (2 Corinthians 5:7). Faith in God's promises comes by hearing God's Words (Romans 10:17). Today, many Christians find it hard to operate in faith because they do not know God's Word regarding their circumstances. Faith begins with the knowledge of God's will, and we obtain this knowledge from hearing God's Word.

True faith believes that something is possible even though it looks impossible in the natural. You know it is truly beyond your natural ability to bring change to the situation. There is absolutely no logic to continue believing in its possibility, but you believe anyway because it is based on God's promises. This is the secret to creating real change in your circumstances.

You have to abandon all reason when you choose to have genuine faith. Your actions will not only seem unreasonable to those around you who see you believing for the impossible but also to your own mind. Your actions might even look irresponsible to those around you. How do you think Abraham felt going around calling himself a father of many nations when he did not even have one child? He must have felt like a foolish old man. But that did not stop him. He believed in God and latched on to the promise of God's Word until he received the promise.

In the same way for your situation, latch on to the promises of God's Word until you see with your eye of faith the picture God has put in your heart. Hold on to it until it manifests for you. The power to walk by faith is in you. If you walk by sight, nothing will change.

Faith Sees And Receives

You have a spiritual inner sight (your spirit man in Christ) who sees everything God has given you. Whatever you desire, use God's Word to take hold of it. Do not dwell on your present situation. Keep your attention on what is already yours because all things are already yours in Christ. The Scripture says that God has already freely given us all things through Jesus (Romans 8:32).

Make no mistake; seeing what God has already provided for you with your inner sight is not an easy process. If it were, everyone you know would be doing it.

It is so much easier to go with the flow, but God asks us to swim *upstream* when everyone else is going downstream. God has called us to stand out, separate ourselves from the crowd and do things differently.

So, when you pray, do you believe what you see on the inside? Do you believe that your visions, dreams, and desires that you want to hold or walk in are possible? Become conscious of the possibilities that are in Christ. For with God, all things are *possible,* and all things are *possible* to those who believe (Mark 9: 23).

Many people push their faith into the future, always in the waiting mode for something to happen, waiting for their prayers to be answered, but God's Word says that faith is NOW. This means you can have the answer to your prayers now. If you can see yourself on the inside possessing the answer or solution to your need now, even though you have not seen it with your physical eyes yet, then it will not be long before you see the manifestation of the answer.

All things are ours to receive now. Why wait? we are already redeemed at the cross. Did we wait to be saved? No, we received salvation through faith in Jesus's death and resurrection, and we were saved. In the same way, at the same time on the cross, Jesus paid the price for everything we will ever need. He paid for salvation, healing, peace of mind, provision, and everything else that pertain to life and godliness. And they are available to us now.

The Scripture says that whatever things we desire, we are to ask for them during prayer, and we are to believe that we have received first and then we will have them (Mark 11: 24). *Whatever things we desire!* This means there are no limits to God's resources and God providing for our needs. We are only limited by our capacity to receive from Him. The only factor that obstructs our receiving is our lack of faith. God is not limited, and He is not withholding anything from us. Our faith in Him will determine the answer, and He will only work according to our faith.

In our circumstances, many a time, we do not see a way out. But when God looks at us, He sees the victory that is ours by His grace. We must look through God's eyes by faith to see how God sees us. God wants us to focus on who He says we are in Christ and receive what is ours through our union with Christ. When we are conscious that we are blessed, healed, redeemed, delivered, and so on in Christ, we will see the manifestation.

Faith Speaks

Faith has a language that it speaks. It is God's language;

it emulates the way God speaks. To walk by faith and receive victory, we must talk like God. The Scripture says, *"By faith, we understand that the universe was formed at God's command so that what is seen was not made out of what was visible"* (Hebrews 11:3, NIV).

So, God created the universe using His words alone. It was all made out of things not visible, meaning invisible stuff was made into the visible universe at the power of God's command. We see this throughout Genesis chapters 1 and 2. God spoke what He wanted to happen. When He wanted light, He said, *"Let there be light, and it was light"* (Genesis 1:3, NIV).

God did not say anything that He did not wish to happen. We also must operate like God and speak only the things that we want to come to pass. James 3:11 teaches that the same fountain cannot spring forth both sweet water and bitter water. Similarly, you cannot speak words of faith and then say words of doubt, negativity, and discouragement in the same breath.

Faith Acts And Overcomes

Many people pray but do not get the desired answers to their prayers. For your desire to manifest, sometimes you must act your faith for others to see. In my introduction to this book, I mentioned how I acted out my faith when I needed a situation in my life to change. I needed to move to a new house but could not afford it. I packed up boxes of belongings I did not use every day, getting ready to move even when I had no idea where I was going or how I would pay for it. Packing up those boxes was my act of faith.

Abraham's act of faith was to call himself a father of many nations even though he did not have a child. Acting your faith may often look foolish, but it will produce results as God sees your faith.

Jesus saw the faith of the paralyzed man and his friends. Their faith compelled them to action, and they wanted to get to Jesus at all costs, even if it meant tearing down the roof of the house that Jesus was staying in (Mark 2: 2-5). Your faith can be seen through the actions that you take. The Scripture says, "*For faith without works is dead*" (James 2:17, NKJV).

Sometimes, after you have done everything you know to do, even then, you may not see the answers to your prayer right away. Then what can you do? It is easy to lose your faith and enthusiasm and become sluggish in your faith during such times of delay. The enemy of your soul starts to apply pressure and starts lying to you that God's Word does not work. He lies that God did not hear you when you prayed or that your situation is impossible to change. But God already knew that there would be times when our faith will have to be followed by patience before we can see the promises manifest. This is the reason God tells us in Scripture not to become sluggish but to imitate those who, through patience and faith, inherit the promises (Hebrews 6:12). This is the time to stand firm and not listen to the lies of the enemy. God is always true to His Word. If you stand your ground, you will inherit the promise and receive the desires of your heart.

Another concept to illustrate faith in action is with the story of the childless Shunammite woman (2 Kings 4:8-37), who was blessed with a child because of Elisha's prophesy that she would be a mother.

Faith Is Calm In The Middle Of The Storm

The Shunammite woman was a woman of faith. You could tell from her actions. She showed much kindness to Elisha, the Prophet, by thoughtfully providing him a place to stay during his visit to her town. He, too, wanted to return her kindness. He came to know that she was childless. So Elisha prophesied that she would have a child, and soon after, she became pregnant and bore a son.

As the child grew, one day, he got sick and died in his mother's arms. Do you know what she did? She did not panic, yell for help, or cause a scene. She did not even tell her husband. There was an answer to this problem, and she was going to find it. There was no time to waste. She knew who had the answer, and she was going to the very source for the solution. When she was asked what was wrong, her response was, "*it is well.*"

She asked her servant to get her transportation ready. She then drove as fast as she could to the place the man of God was staying, her face like flint. The man of God saw her from far away, and the Scripture says he told his servant, "*Please run now to meet her, and say to her, 'Is it well with you? Is it well with your husband? Is it well with the child?' And she answered, "It is well"* (2 Kings 4:26, NKJV).

When she reached the man of God and told him that her child was dead, he was going to send his servant to go with her, but she was not going to settle for second best. She wanted the man of God himself to come to deal with the situation. The man of God represented God Himself, and only his presence would do. It turns out that she was right. Her faith and unwavering determination to be victorious in this matter helped her child. The child eventually came back to life.

What can we learn from this story? We learned that faith refuses to believe what it sees in the natural realm. It places its trust and chooses to believe God in the middle of a storm because God can do the impossible. As we see, the woman chose to believe the God of Elisha and was careful with her words and only declared the result that she wanted to see. She kept stating, "It is well," and it turned out well for her.

Faith always overcomes, whatever the circumstances may be. The Shunammite woman did not let herself consider the situation in her natural mind. She set her mind on the fact that her child was a gift from God in the first place, and God would not take him away from her. She had a positive confession that it was well. Her heart and the words of her mouth were in agreement with God's Word.

You may be in a situation today that looks hopeless. Maybe the doctor has said there is no hope for you. Perhaps you need a financial miracle to make it through to the end of the month. Perhaps you are dealing with an anguishing emotional issue. Whatever the situation, run to the One who has the answer, and He will help you. The Scripture says, *"Let us, therefore, come boldly to the throne of grace, that we may obtain mercy and find grace to help in time of need"* (Hebrews 4:16, NKJV).

Faith says there is an answer. I may not see it now, but I know it is there. I will stand on the Word until I see the manifestation of the promise! Use the affirmations below to renew your mind and build your faith by repeating the faith scriptures.

AFFIRMATIONS FOR A LIFE OF FAITH

I trust in the LORD, my God, with all my heart; I do not depend on my own understanding

— PROVERBS 3:5

By grace, I am saved through faith; and that not of myself: it is the gift of God

— EPHESIANS 2:8

I walk and live by faith, not by my physical sight

— 2 CORINTHIANS 5:7

God is my refuge and strength, my ever-present help in times of trouble

— PSALM 46:1

I am saved now by grace through faith in Jesus. It is not because of anything that I have done

— EPHESIANS 2:8-9

God can do far above everything that I asked or imagined according to his power that is working in me

— EPHESIANS 3:20

I am blessed because I believe: for there shall be a performance of those things which were told me from the Lord

— LUKE 1:45

By faith, I know that the world and the stars and everything else were made at God's command; and that they were all created from things that cannot be seen

— HEBREWS 11:3

Faith is the confidence that what I am hoping for will actually happen; it gives me assurance about things I cannot see

— HEBREWS 11:1

I choose to act on my faith because faith without works is dead
— JAMES 2:17

So, then faith comes to me by hearing the Word of God

— ROMANS 10:17

I am righteous and justified, and l live by faith

— ROMANS 1:17

8

A GRATEFUL HEART

"We all have circumstances and times when we may be tempted to complain, but find something to be grateful for instead. Studies show that people who practice gratefulness are happier people!"

— VICTORIA OSTEEN

Scripture Reading:

"Enter into His gates with thanksgiving, and into His courts with praise; be thankful unto him and bless His name"

— PSALM. 100:4, NIV

Thankfulness Is Good

Many people only think about giving thanks during the Thanksgiving holidays. They forget all the blessings and goodness of God towards them every day the rest of the year and assume they have everything they need because they worked hard for it. Giving thanks and being grateful should be an everyday practice in our lives, starting from the moment we wake up.

Expressing thankfulness and gratitude to God is essential. Thanksgiving is a way of acknowledging what God has done and is presently doing. We also thank Him for things not yet manifested because we know that God has already accomplished everything for us in the spirit.

We all have dreams, desires, and goals that we believe to receive or achieve, and often, we must wait for them to come to pass. Thanking God in advance for the promise is a quick way to bring the manifestation of your desires. The scripture says the person who offers thanksgiving as his sacrifice brings glory to God (Psalm 50:23).

We must develop an attitude of thanksgiving and gratitude, no matter our situation in life. Sometimes we have everything we need and still are not thankful. We can see that happening in our society right now. Some people have so much but are not grateful to God for them.

Others who do not have enough complain that they have too little. The Bible talks about how the children of Israel complained about their situation in the wilderness, even after everything God had done for them.

While they were slaves in Egypt, being overworked by their masters, they cried out to God, and He did mighty miracles for them and brought them into the desert as a free people. When they were sojourning to the promised land flowing with milk and honey, God fed them every day with manna (divine food) for forty years. He protected them from the scorching desert sun with a pillar of cloud during the day and from the cold desert wind with a pillar of fire during the night. God protected them so that no one among them was sick and no other nation attacked them, yet they complained. Their behavior made God angry after everything He had done for them.

Some of us are like those Israelites of old today. We often forget the blessings that God pours into our lives day by day. We complain about our government, our economies, jobs, bosses and co-workers, our church, our spouses, children, what they are not doing right, and so on. Complaining about those things will not change them. Real change only happens when we start replacing our complaints with words of gratitude and thankfulness to God despite the situation we find we find ourselves in.

Intentional Gratitude

The scripture says, *"Let them give thanks to the Lord for his unfailing love and his wonderful deeds for mankind, for he satisfies the thirsty and fills the hungry with good things"* (Psalm 107:8-9, NIV).

Our gratitude should be intentional because our natural tendency is to be ungrateful. We often want to overlook the good and focus on the negative. Hence we must intentionally recognize all that we have been blessed with and consciously express our gratitude to God because an attitude of gratitude pleases God. The Scripture says, *"In everything, give thanks: for this is the will of God in Christ Jesus concerning you"* (1 Thessalonians 5:18, KJV).

Being grateful is God's will for us. We should say thank you to God all the time, both when things are going well and when things are not going according to plan. We must cultivate the habit of being intentionally grateful, just like the psalmist did. In Psalm 103:1-5, The Psalmist asks us to remember all of God's benefits and all the good things the Lord has done for us.

Thanking God often reminds us of who God is, how great He really is and how much we are dependent on Him. Even when things look bleak in the natural, there is always light because God is light. The light of God will shine into your situation, light your path, and show you what you need to do.

The Bible encourages the people of God to give thanks to God because He is good. We often say God is a good God. We see His goodness surround us every day. His Mercies endures forever, and He is faithful. When we think about all the Lord had done for us and all that He promises to do, and we think about His attributes, His awesomeness, His greatness and then realize that this Almighty, Great, and Wonderful God is in love with us! Oh, that will make us want to rejoice and sing praises like the psalmist, *"O give thanks unto the Lord; for He is good: for his mercy endures forever"* (Psalm 136:1, NKJV).

Thanksgiving and gratitude are spiritual ways to combat worry, anxiety, negative thoughts and help you keep believing what God has said. Abraham gave God glory and thanked God for the promise long before getting the child he believed for (Romans 4:20). Worrying saps your spiritual strength and weakens your faith while having a grateful attitude keeps your faith strong.

Always being grateful helps you focus on God instead of your circumstances and helps you walk in the spirit instead of focusing on the flesh. Focusing on God will align your spirit man with God's Spirit so that you will receive the answer you need from the Spirit of God. Philippians 4:6-7 says we should pray about everything instead of being anxious. Anxiety and negative emotions are removed when you give thanks and praise to God for the situation you are dealing with.

Gratitude And Thanksgiving Are Powerful

We see how the power of praising and thanking God was demonstrated whenever Israel went to battle against one of its enemies. In one of these instances, the enemy's army came to make war with Israel. This enemy was more powerful than Israel. So, as directed by the Spirit of God to King Jehoshaphat, the battle plan was that they sing praises and give thanks to God instead of fighting. Scripture says He asked them to praise God because of His glory and holiness and to give thanks to the Lord God because of His faithfulness (2 Chronicles 20:21). When they did this, their enemy was defeated before them.

When Jesus walked on earth, We see Him expressed gratitude for the little that they had in the time when it looked like there was insufficiency. He had five thousand hungry mouths to feed with only five loaves and two small fishes! Scripture says Jesus gave thanks for the five loaves of bread and two fishes and then asked the disciples to give them to the people. The people ate as much bread and fishes as they wanted, and there were lots of leftovers (John 6:11). Jesus gave thanks to the Father, who is the source of all things, and miracles happened.

Thank God during times of trouble, difficulty, and insufficiency. We give thanks to God not for the issues and problems we are facing but in spite of them because God does not bring troubles to us. Thanksgiving helps us submit to His will and allows us to trust Him. Even when we do not understand what is going on or why things are the way they are, we can trust God and put our faith in His word. We can express our thanksgiving to him, and God will help us. The scripture says, *"Always giving thanks to God the Father for everything, in the name of our Lord Jesus Christ"* (Ephesians 5:20, NIV).

Jesus taught us the importance of gratitude through the story of the ten lepers who came to Him for healing. Naturally, Jesus healed them all and asked them to go and show themselves to the priest to prove they were healed, as was the tradition in those days. When the lepers followed Jesus's instructions, they were healed. One of them was so happy and excited that he returned to Jesus to say thank you. And he was a Samaritan! So, Jesus answered and said, *"Were there not ten cleansed?*

But where are the nine? Were there not any found who returned to give glory to God except this foreigner?" And He said to him, "Arise, go your way. Your faith has made you well" (Luke 17:11-19, NIV).

Imagine that! Nine other lepers had also been healed of a debilitating illness, but they did not return to give thanks to Jesus. And to the one that did return, Jesus amplified his healing. He was not just cured but was made well. Let us not be like those nine lepers who did not express their gratitude to Jesus.

Let us remember every day to be thankful for what God has done and what He is doing for us. He has blessed, healed, and given us peace. We are unconditionally loved; Jesus died for us and redeemed us so that we are now sons and daughters of God. He promised never to leave us but to always be with us. Oh my! So much to be thankful for every day! So now it is time for affirmation scriptures to help beautify your mind as you continue to express your gratitude for being a chosen child of God, who is saved, healed, delivered, justified, and sanctified by the cross of our Lord.

AFFIRMATIONS FOR A GRATEFUL HEART

Whatever I do, in word or action, I do everything in the name of Jesus, giving thanks to God the Father through Jesus my Lord

— COLOSSIANS 3:17

I give thanks to the Lord, for He is good; His love endures forever

— 1 CHRONICLES 16:34

I always thank my God for everyone because of His grace given to me in Christ Jesus

— 1 CORINTHIANS 1:4

I refuse to be anxious about anything, but in every situation, by prayer and petition, with thanksgiving, I present my petitions to God. And the peace of God that is beyond all understanding guards my heart and mind in Christ Jesus

— PHILIPPIANS 4:6-7

The Lord is my shield and my strength. My heart trusts in Him, and I am helped. I exult Him with my song, and I give thanks to him

— PSALM 28:7

I praise the name of God with songs; I will exalt Him with Thanksgiving

— PSALM 69:30

I will sing of the Lord's great love forever; with my mouth, I will make your faithfulness known to all generations. I will declare that your love stands steadfast forever, that you have established your faithfulness in heaven itself

— PSALM 89:1-2

I will enter His gates with thanksgiving and His courts with praise; I will give thanks to the Lord and praise His name

— PSALM 100:4

I give thanks to the Lord for his unfailing love and his wonderful deeds for mankind. He fills the hungry ones with good things and satisfies the thirsty

— PSALM 107:8-9

I always rejoice. I pray without ceasing. I give thanks in all circumstances, for this is the will of God in Christ Jesus for me

— 1 THESSALONIANS 5:16-18

I sing loud praise and worship to God, and I thank Him

— PSALM 92: 1-5

God inhabits my praises because I am His child

— PSALM 22:3

Now thanks be to God who always leads me in triumph

— 2 CORINTHIANS 2:14

9

HELP AND GUIDANCE

"Don't look at yourself and say, "Will God help me? Am I good enough?" Put aside such thoughts and express your faith in Him."

— DAVID O. OYEDEPO

S **cripture Reading:**

"I will lift up my eyes to the mountains; From where shall my help come? My help comes from the LORD, Who made heaven and earth"

— PSALM 121:1,2, NIV

Lord, I Need Help!

As Christians, we ask God for help every day, consciously or unconsciously, because He promised to help and guide us when we ask. He is a very present and reliable help in times of trouble. Some people say they do not want to bother God with the little things in their life. They feel God may not like to be disturbed with trifles which they can take care of themselves. But this is not how God wants to relate with us. He loves us and invites us to come to Him with whatever we need, and He promised to help us with everything, both the big and important things and in the little things as well. The scripture says, The Lord hears and delivers His people from trouble when they call unto Him for help (Psalm 34:17).

There are many reasons why we call unto the Lord for help and guidance, but it is often because we cannot figure out stuff ourselves. We mostly only ask for His help and direction after making a mess of everything, and then we ask Him to fix things for us. God is our ever-present help, and He helps us when we ask.

We have all heard of Jabez, whose name meant "sorrow" because his mother had felt much pain while giving birth to him. So, because his name meant sorrow, he was a sorrowful man. Nothing in his life was going well until he he called out to God for help, and boy, did God help him! The Scripture says, *"And Jabez called on the God of Israel saying, 'Oh, that You would bless me indeed, and enlarge my territory, that Your hand would be with me, and that You would keep me from evil, that I may not cause pain!' So, God granted him what he requested"* (1 Chronicles 4:10, NKJV).

God gave Jabez everything he asked for in prayer. We know that God is not a respecter of persons (Acts 10:34). If He helped Jabez when he asked for help, He will help you too, but you must ask. He answers those who ask, and He shows them great and might things (Jeremiah 33:3).

We see throughout the Bible how much God loves and cares for His people. He helped, guided, and protected the children of Israel from their enemies while they were sojourning in the desert. As His children, God promises to continue to guide and protect us from our enemies. He gave us the Holy Spirit to teach, lead and guide us so that we end up in the correct destination for us all the time (John 16:13).

Sometimes, we are guided by our feelings and emotions, and we make decisions based on them. Decisions based on our emotions and feelings often turn out to be very biased against God's word and will for our lives. Instead, our relationship with God and His love for us should be the basis of our getting direction, help, and guidance from Him. In Isaiah 48:17, God says that He will teach us what is best for us and direct us in the way we should go. He will tell us the right way or path to take, whether to go left or right (Isaiah 30:21). So when we are guided by our relationship with God and His love for us, we will not lose our way in the wilderness of life.

As a Christian, if you are not guided by God in your life decisions, who guides you, and from whom do you get your instructions? Do you go about life depending on yourself, what you see around you, and what you have seen others experience? Proverbs 3:6 says He will direct your paths if you acknowledge Him in all your ways. He will instruct you and lead you in the way that you should go (Psalm 32:8).

God always keeps His promises. He said He would instruct, guide you and help you. He will tell you what steps to take and what things to avoid so that you can get to your destination in life, have your needs met, or receive the answers you want.

Holy Spirit-Our Inner GPS

As Christians, we sometimes make a huge mess of things, and we wonder how we can get ourselves into such a mess in life, especially when we call the Lord our God. This happens when we have not asked God for help or listened to the voice of the Holy Spirit and His leading on the inside.

How do we know what the Holy Spirit is saying to us? Jesus said that His sheep hears His voice (John 10:27), and Jesus is always shepherding His sheep because He is the Good Shepherd. He is constantly speaking to us and guiding us. Do you remember ever having an intuition about something or a hunch, but you ignored it, and things went sour? That was the Lord trying to get your attention. This has happened to me several times, and I am sure to most Christians as well.

Since Jesus is your Lord, you have an inbuilt guiding system in you. I call it your inner GPS. God has given the Holy Spirit to lead and guide you. God knows precisely who you are and what you are going through. He has given you the scriptures and the Holy Spirit to guide you to make sure you are following the right path.

In the old testament, we see how God delivered the children of Israel out of bondage. He guided them through the wilderness and into the promised land using physical means and prophets because they did not have the Bible to guide them at that time.

For us, Jesus promised that we would not be left alone, but He would send us guidance and help in the form of the Holy Spirit, who will tell us what the Father has said. Jesus wants us to be consciously aware that we have a guiding system on the inside. If we become consciously aware of His presence, we will always depend on Him to help lead and guide us.

God Guides Us Through His Word

It takes strength and courage to walk with God and follow His direction, especially when you have pressures of life coming at you from all sides while trying to make decisions. The Scripture says that God told Joshua not to be afraid but to be strong and have the courage to follow His commands in the midst of difficult circumstances (Joshua 1:9). He knew that Joshua was under pressure after Moses' death and had no idea how to lead the Israelites into the promised land. Yet, though the pressures were real and he had to make tough decisions, God was with him to help him with clear and accurate guidance whenever he needed it.

Similarly, by the grace of our Lord Jesus Christ, we can find direction in the Bible for any and every area of our lives as well. We can clarify which direction to go and what decision to make with the Holy Spirit's help.

God promises to guide, teach and instruct us so that we will always know the right path to follow (Psalm 32:8).

As God often directs us through His Word, we must always ensure that we are knowledgeable in the Word of God. So the importance of studying the Word of God every day and meditating on it cannot be over-emphasized. That is how we receive direction for the steps we must take. I have heard people say they asked God for help or asked God about something, but He did not answer. God always hears and answers when we call on Him, but sometimes we do not like the answers because it is not what we want, so we reject it and say God did not respond. God always keeps His promises, hears, and answers us when we pray in faith.

Illogical Direction

God said He would help you through challenging, hopeless, and desperate times of your life. Even when everyone has abandoned you, God promises that He will never leave you or forsake you. He promises to be with you to guide you and tell you what to do about the situation you are facing. Sometimes, what He asks you to do may not be logical, but following through will yield boundless blessings. So, we should always endeavor to do what the spirit of God asks us to do even if we do not know why we should do it that way and even when it does not make sense.

We see how God led Joshua to march around the city of Jericho for seven days. It did not make sense. How can marching around a city for seven days be a battle plan and bring down a fortified city? God commanded Joshua to appoint seven priests to carry trumpets of rams' horns in front of the ark. On the seventh day, they were to march around the city seven times, with the priests blowing the trumpets. When the priests sound a long blast of praise on the trumpets, the whole army was to give a very loud shout; then, the walls of the city would collapse, and the army could go up, and everyone straight in. Even though it sounded crazy, Joshua and the people of Israel followed God's command anyway. They shouted as God commanded on the seventh day, and God brought the walls of the great fortified city crashing down. Israel got their victory because Joshua listened to God's guidance (Joshua 6:1-20).

Sometimes there may be no wrong or right decisions in some of the situations that we face. This is the reason God asks us to seek His wisdom. We need His wisdom to ensure that we are following the best course of action for our situations. So the best way is to ask

God for enlightenment and wisdom in whatever situation we are facing. God says He will counsel us with His eye. God loves us, and He advises us because He wants the best life for us. We accept His guidance because of our loving and trusting relationship with Him, and of course, we want everything to go well with us. Thus it is essential not to make decisions based on your knowledge and wisdom, even if it sounds like the logical thing to do. God knows and sees everything. He sees the end from the beginning, and He knows what is best for you.

God asks us not to be stubborn like the horse or the mule, which must be bridled to make them obey. We should willingly submit to and obey God's instructions and follow His guidance. When God's counsel is ignored, and we live life in rebellion, the consequences can be unpleasant.

At times, you may fail in an endeavor, maybe due to disobedience to God's Word or not seeking God's direction, whatever the reasons may be. In such a case, when you have come to your senses, do not sweat it. Repent and move on, remembering that God's loving-kindness surrounds you always. Ask His forgiveness and His help at such times. Then stay close to Jesus so that he can direct all your actions, and He will give you the grace to deal with the consequences of your decisions. Doing this will get you back on track to following and listening to God's instructions. The Scripture says, *"The salvation of the righteous comes from the Lord; he is their stronghold in time of trouble. The Lord helps them and delivers them; he delivers them from the wicked and saves them, because they take refuge in him"* (Psalm 37:39-40, NIV).

We need God always. When things are going well, and when they are not going so well. We need God's guidance to keep things going well or help us get out of whatever mess we have made. God is the one who delivers us out of the tight spaces that we sometimes find ourselves in (Psalm 18:2), and He loves doing it too. We have a good God and Father.

The Scripture affirmations below were chosen to help develop your faith and renew your mind in the area of seeking God's help and guidance. Declare them to beautify your mind and build up your inner man, to overcome in every area of your life.

AFFIRMATIONS FOR HELP AND GUIDANCE

I am happy because I have the God of Jacob as my Helper, and my hope is in the LORD my God

— PSALM 146:5

I will not fear because the Lord is with me; I will not be discouraged because the Lord is my God. He will strengthen me; yes, He will help me, He will uphold me with His righteous right hand

— ISAIAH 41:10

The LORD is my Redeemer, the Holy One of Israel: He is the LORD my God, who lectures me on what is best for me, who directs me in the way I should go

— ISAIAH 48:17

My help comes from the Almighty God, who made the heavens and earth

— PSALM 121:2

The LORD answers me when I call to Him because I fear Him, and He delivers me.

— PSALM 34:7

The Lord instructs me and teaches me in the way that I should go. He guides me with His eye

— PSALM 32:8

I seek the LORD, and He answers me; He delivered me from all my fears

— PSALM 34:4

The Lord shows me the right path and points out the right road for me to follow

— PSALM 25:4

God is my refuge and strength, my very present help in trouble

— PSALM 46:1

I am Jesus's sheep. I hear His voice, and I follow Him

— JOHN 10:27

My Helper is the Holy Spirit, whom the Father has sent in the name of Jesus. He teaches me everything and brings to my remembrance all things that Jesus said

— JOHN 14:26

The Lord will never leave me nor forsake me. So, I boldly say, The LORD is my helper, so I will not fear what man can do to me

— HEBREWS 13:5-6

The Lord is my Shepherd; I shall have no lack or want. He makes me lie down in green and luscious pastures. He leads me beside still waters. He restores my soul. He leads me in righteous paths for His name's sake

— PSALM 23: 1-3

NO FEAR HERE

"I don't worry; I don't fear; I know that God is on my side."

— BENSON ANDREW IDAHOSA

S**cripture Reading**:
   "Do not be afraid, for I am with you. Do not be discouraged, for I am your God. I will strengthen you and help you. I will hold you up with my victorious right hand"

— ISAIAH 41:10, NLT

Fear Is A Spirit

The situation in the world is deteriorating, causing many people to be fearful and anxious. There is the fear of diseases, fear of domestic and international terrorism, and fears due to economic downturns. People are afraid of losing everything they own, from their homes, jobs, other sources of income to their lifestyle. Fear rules the hearts of many, as they see no sign of hope in troubled times. Even the news is flooded with negative reports, which heightens the fear and anxiety of many.

Though people often try to manage their fear by hiding it, laughing about it or denying it, this is not the correct response to alleviate fear and anxiety. The Bible teaches us that fear is a spirit and must not be welcomed into our lives because it is not from God. The Scripture says, *"God has not given us a spirit of fear, but of power and love and a sound mind"* (2 Timothy 1:7, NKJV).

The Spirit God has given us makes us bold instead of cowardly. God is our strength and our song. He is our shield, our strong tower in whom we take refuge. Knowing God's unchangeable nature emboldens us, making us brave, fearless children of God. However, we must remember that this power to be courageous is not our own doing but the work of God inside us.

There are two types of fear, namely, good and bad fear. Good fear is the kind that acknowledges God, has holy respect (fear for Him and honors Him. Good fear is the kind that the Bible encourages us to have. God gave the law to the children of Israel so that they would learn to fear Him, and it was for their good. The Scripture says, *"So the Lord commanded us to observe all these statutes, to fear the Lord our God for our good always and for our survival, as it is today* (Deuteronomy 6:24, NIV).

Bad fear fills people with dread and stops them from doing what they should do. It is often the spirit behind some forms of procrastination. It clouds your mind, so you cannot concentrate. It stifles your ability to think clearly and paralyzes your ability to make decisions because fear is ungodly. Fear is not a part of your born-again spirit. It is a spirit of bondage. The Scripture says, *"For ye have not received the spirit of bondage again to fear; but ye have received the Spirit of adoption, whereby we cry, Abba, Father"* (Romans 8:15, KJV).

Fight Fear With God's Word

Fear often arises from ignorance, so that we fear what we do not know or understand. The enemy of our souls usually uses our ignorance to feed and incite our imagination. Thus, he takes away our God-given vision and makes us picture things going wrong and our life situations worsening, which in turn cuts off our faith. The image that God gives us through His Word is filled with hope and revives our hearts. However, the vision that fear presents is full of confusion, discouragement, and hopelessness. When we accept it into our hearts, it causes our spiritual growth to be stifled, and we begin to reverse our spiritual course. We start to hear the enemy's voice on the inside more than the voice of God, and then, we become slaves to our fears.

God encourages his people not to fall victim to fear. There are so many scriptures in the Bible where God tells His people that there is no need to be afraid or be worried because He is our God, and He is with us. The word of God often removes any ignorance or any condition that produces fear in our lives when we read it. Scripture says, *"The entrance of Your words gives light; it gives understanding to the simple"* (Psalm 119:130, NKJV).

God is love. And there is no fear in love. Fear does not exist where there is perfect love (1 John 4:18). God's love for us is unconditional and perfect. He cannot help but love us because He is love and His nature is love. We can never do anything that will make Him not love us anymore. His love for us is sealed, and we experience God's love through Jesus because Jesus is the visible expression of God's love for us.

We are never distant from God. He is always with us, and He is in us, so we do not need to fear. We may feel removed and distant, but that is our mind lying to us. The truth is what God's Word says. God will never leave us. The Scripture says, *"I have chosen you and have not rejected you. So do not fear, for I am with you; do not be dismayed, for I am your God. I will strengthen you and help you; I will uphold you with my righteous right hand"* (Isaiah 41:9-10, NIV).

The enemy uses fear of the future and fear of unfulfilled hopes and dreams to make us feel down and bad about ourselves. We need not fear tomorrow, for our future is in His hands. God promises life, protection, provision, and deliverance to the person who fears the Lord.

The scripture affirmations in this chapter will help you break free from any paralyzing grips of fear you may have in your life. Meditate on them and boldly declare them to beautify your mind so that you can see the victory that you believe for.

NO FEAR HERE AFFIRMATIONS

My fear of the Lord leads me to life so that I may sleep satisfied, untouched by evil

— PROVERBS 19:23

God tells me to be strong and of good courage. I will not be terrified or discouraged, for the LORD my God is with me, wherever I go

— JOSHUA 1:9

I am not afraid, for God is my shield and my exceeding great reward

— GENESIS 15:1

The LORD, my God, takes hold of my right hand and tells me not to fear; He is my helper

— ISAIAH 41:13

*I will not be afraid of bad news; because
my heart is steadfast, trusting in the Lord*

— PSALM 112:7

*The angel of the Lord makes camp around
me because I fear the Lord, and He rescues
me*

— PSALM 34:7

*He fulfills my desires because I fear Him;
He hears my cry and saves me*

— PSALM 145:19

Whenever I am afraid, I put my trust in you

— PSALM 56:3

I fear the Lord, and He prolongs my life

— PROVERBS 10:27

Because I fear His name, the sun of righteousness will rise with healing in its wings; and I will go forward skipping about like a calf from the stall

— MALACHI 4:2

I did not receive the Spirit that puts me in bondage to fear, but I received the Spirit of adoption, and through Him, I cry out, "Abba, Father"

— ROMANS 8:15

Praise the Lord! I am blessed because I fear the Lord and greatly delight in His commandments

— PSALM 112:1

God has chosen me and has not rejected me. So I do not fear, for God is with me; I am not dismayed, for the Lord is my God.

— ISAIAH 41:9

11

LORD, TEACH US TO PRAY

"You can pray without faith, but you cannot have faith without being a man of prayer."

— AROME OSAYI

Scripture Reading:

"So I say to you: Ask, and it will be given to you; seek, and you will find; knock and the door will be opened to you. For everyone who asks receives; the one who seeks finds; and to the one who knocks, the door will be opened".

— LUKE 11:9-13, NIV

How Not To Pray

Christians and people worldwide pray every day for God to help them solve their problems. But, most of these people do not genuinely believe or expect to receive answers to their prayers. Many pray out of religious obligation, while others pray as the last resort when everything else they tried has failed them. With a defeated attitude, they say, all else has failed; let us pray! For some other Christians, prayer is the start of an arduous journey, which draws into a big, long spiritual fight. It culminates into an even longer waiting period to get results, if at all!

Sometimes we pray and are not even sure if God heard our prayers. Even if we think He heard, we are not convinced He will answer. When we pray, we try to convince God about the gravity of the circumstances and conditions we find ourselves in and implore him to help us.

We repeatedly pray in the same manner, day in and day out, because we are not convinced He heard us the first time. Often when praying, we try to make Him change His mind by our eloquence, our heartfelt pleas, and our tears. The scriptures say we often ask amiss. *"You do not have because you do not ask. You ask and do not receive because you ask amiss"* (James 4:3, NKJV).

Sometimes, to cover our basis, we go into the 'in case He does not hear me, He might listen to you' mentality. We form prayer chains because we assume that others are more righteous than us, and somehow, their prayers will be answered because they are more blessed than us. Make no mistake, asking others to agree with us in prayers over our situations and the things that trouble us is a righteous and biblical thing to do. Jesus said that if any two believers agree in prayer, they will receive what they prayed for (Matthew 18:19). But our prayers are not answered because the prayers of one hundred people are more potent than that of just one or two believers.

Teach Us To Pray Right

The disciples of Jesus found themselves in a challenging situation one day when they tried to heal a possessed boy but could not cure him. They had prayed and done everything they had seen Jesus do before, but they did not get the same results Jesus would get (Matthew 17: 14-18).

This brings to mind the story of the prophet Elijah and the prophets of Baal. Elijah had issued a challenge that whichever God answers by fire is the real God. The prophets of Baal prayed and carried out all their rituals from morning to evening. Still, no answer was forthcoming to their prayers. Elijah mocked them at this point. The Scripture says, *"And so it was, at noon, that Elijah mocked them and said, "Cry aloud, for he is a god; either he is meditating, or he is busy, or he is on a journey, or perhaps he is sleeping and must be awakened"* (1 Kings 18:27, NKJV).

But they got no answers to their prayers. When it was Elijah's turn, he called on the Lord, and God answered in an instant. He sent fire down to consume the offerings even though they were soaking wet. This incident proved to the people that the God of Elijah was the real God (1 Kings 18:20-40, NKJV).

Many Christians are like the disciples of Jesus or like the prophets of Baal in their prayers. They pray ritualistically to a God who they do not personally know. They pray because it is the norm to pray when something goes wrong or because the priest asked them to pray, or they grew up in a Christian home where mom and dad always prayed. Prayers of this sort most often miss the mark and do not get results. Jesus rebuked His disciples when they could not heal the boy, saying their faith was little and they needed to grow their faith to manifest certain miracles (Matthew 17:20). They did not honestly believe that they would get the answer they were looking for.

The disciples of Jesus observed Jesus's life, how He often prayed, setting Himself apart on a mountain or a private corner to pour out His heart to the Father the whole night long. On one such occasion, after Jesus returned from praying, one of the disciples asked Jesus to teach them to pray (Luke 11:1). That is when Jesus taught them the Lord's prayer, starting with 'Our Father' (Luke 11:2-4).

Prayer Based on Relationship

Jesus' teaching on prayer begs the question, 'What is prayer?' I mean the kind of prayers that God hears and that gets answers? The type of prayer that brings results has its foundation in a relationship with the Father through Jesus.

Our prayers will get results when we consciously know that we are in a relationship with God the Father through Jesus. We are daughters and sons of our great God, and our sins are forgiven through Jesus' death on the cross, and we are loved. Knowing that we have access to the Father always and are always welcomed in His presence is the key to getting our prayers answered. Knowledge of and the assurance produced by our relationship with the Father through Jesus increases faith in our hearts.

As children of God, we know that all things are ours now, for the Father has given us everything pertaining to life and Godliness (2 Peter 1:3). He has blessed us and promised to hear us when we call on Him. *"This is the confidence we have in approaching God: that if we ask anything according to his will, he hears us. And if we know that he hears us—whatever we ask—we know that we have what we asked of him"* (1 John 5:14-15, NIV).

God is a good Father, and He is good to all. When you believe and pray in line with His word and your request is in line with His will, your prayer will get results. But how do you know that what you are praying for is in line with His will, you ask? Good question! If what you are asking for in prayer is not going to hurt or take something away from someone else but is in line with what is true, honorable, just, pure, and lovely, you can be sure it is in line with His will.

We cannot force God to answer our prayers. We cannot do enough good works to make Him hear us, and it does not matter how dire our situations may be. We cannot guilt Him to answer us. He will not answer us because we prayed longer or fasted for a long time. God deals with us based on His love and His grace alone through faith in Jesus. He only responds to His words and His promises to us. Thus, our prayers and fasting must be based on this foundation of God's grace through faith.

Therefore, we must renew and beautify our minds with the word of God so that we can know what God's Word says about our situation and pray in line with it to receive the answers we need. He said we should call upon Him, and He will answer us and show us great things we did not know before (Jeremiah 33:3). He will help us bring our desires that seem so far away to our now; that is, He will actually give us our desires and not just have us daydreaming and wishing for them to happen.

God will never fail us. He is faithful to His word. If He has done it for someone else, past, or present, He will do it for you. Your situation is not unique. Children of God all over the world are praying and getting victories every day; why not you? If whatever you desire is in line with what God promised, then you have a blank check. He said: *"And I will do whatever you ask in my name, so that the Father may be glorified in the Son"* (John 14:13, NIV).

If your heart can see, believe, and receive what you have asked for in prayers, then it's yours. God is faithful to His promise, and His promises are to us 'Yes and Amen' in Christ (2 Corinthians 1:20).

How To Receive Answers To Prayers

As I already mentioned above, before receiving anything in the natural realm, you have to accept your miracle in your spirit first. It is only when you allow yourself to see it in your mind's eye, take hold of it, see it as yours that you get it in reality. If you cannot appropriate your desire in your mind, you cannot have it in reality.

Consider Hannah for a moment. She wanted, above all, to have a child. Year after year, she could not conceive, whereas her counterpart bore many children. One particular year, her whole family had come to Shiloh to worship. She was so heartbroken because she did not have a child that she went into the temple in the morning to pray her heart out. The priest thought she was drunk and rebuked her for it, but Hannah told Eli, the priest, she was pouring her heart out to the Lord. The priest (who represented the Word of God in those days because they did not have Bibles) told her that God would grant her desires. This made Hannah very happy. She took that word to heart. After that, she cleaned her face, dried her tears, and went to enjoy the feast for the first time in years. Nine months later, Hannah delivered a baby boy just as the priest Eli had spoken, and she was extremely delighted to be a mother (1 Samuel 1-20).

Hannah allowed her heart (her inner man) to receive what Eli spoke to her before receiving the answer she wanted in the natural realm. How do we know that she allowed her heart to receive? Because she was no longer sorrowful. That was an act of faith. She went and enjoyed herself at the feast. As far as she was concerned, it was done. Her believe her prayers were already answered. She was a mother even though she was not even pregnant yet. She accepted the result as hers right now. Eventually, she became a mother of not just one but many children.

When we accept the answer to our prayers as already ours and see the situation as already taken care of by God, we will have what we seek in reality. Doing this communicates our faith and trust in God. When God sees our heart of trust and our total dependence on Him, He is pleased by it. He said in Hebrews 11:6 that it is impossible to please God without faith.

It is this childlike faith that gives us that which we seek in reality. For example, you have bills due but no money to pay them. You need a good job but have not found one, or you want to own your own home and cannot afford it, or you want physical relief from your pain and have not gotten it. Remember that the word of God says, *"Whatever you ask for in prayer, believe that believe that you have have received it, and it will be yours"* (Mark 11:24, NIV).

So, just like Hannah, if you can see it on the inside as yours—you will have, hold and enjoy it in the natural realm. So instead of seeing bills and no money to pay them, pray about it. The scriptures say, *"Do not be anxious about anything, but in every situation, by prayer and petition, with thanksgiving, present your requests to God"* (Philippians 4:6, NIV).

After praying, allow yourself to receive the answer you want, that is, accept with gladness that your bills have already been paid. Accepting anything else will produce fear, worry, and anxiety. If your heart is unable to receive it, do not give up. Meditate on the promise of God until your heart accepts that your bills are paid, or that you got a fantastic job, or that you have the house you want, or that you are healed from pain. This is a spiritual process. As soon as your heart accepts it, the answer will manifest in the natural realm for you.

Pray the prayer of faith once and stay in thanksgiving until you receive the manifestation of your miracle. You do not need to pray, again and again, begging God to hear you. He has already heard, and He has already blessed you through Jesus and given you all things that pertain to life.

Doubt and fear will try to creep into your heart to hinder your faith and stop your fruit from manifesting, hence the importance of developing a beautiful mind. You must guard your heart against all the negative thoughts and attacks of the enemy by continuing to declare God's Word, which is the foundation for your faith. This is the Kingdom's way of having your needs met. Jesus asked us not to worry or be anxious about anything but to seek the Kingdom of God first (Matthew 6:28-34). If you do this, then God promised He would supply all your needs.

The scriptures below will help renew your mind and develop a beautiful mind in you in the areas of praying to receive. Quote them and meditate on them repeatedly until you know on the inside that your prayers are answered even before you have prayed them.

AFFIRMATIONS FOR TEACH US TO PRAY

I call on the Lord, and He answers me; He is with me in times of trouble, He delivers me and honors me

— PSALM 91:15

I abide in Jesus, and His words abide in me, I ask what I will, and it is done for me

— 1 JOHN 15:7

I trust in the LORD forever: for in my LORD JEHOVAH is everlasting strength

— ISAIAH 26:4

It is better for me to put my trust in the LORD than to put confidence in man

— PSALM 118:8

I call unto the Lord, and He answers me and shows me great things that I did not know before

— JEREMIAH 33:3

I pray in the Spirit with all kinds of prayers and requests on all occasions

— EPHESIANS 6:18

*All things are possible to me because I
believe*

— MARK 9:23

*I call upon the Lord and pray to
Him, and He hears me*

— JEREMIAH 29:12

*And whatever I ask in prayer, I receive
because I have faith in God*

— MATTHEW 21:22

*I confidently draw near to the throne of
grace, where I receive mercy and find grace
to help me in my time of need*

— HEBREWS 4:16

*I ask, and it is given to me; I seek, and I
find; I knock, and the door is opened to me*

— MATTHEW 7:7

And this is the confidence that I have toward Him, that if I ask anything according to His will, He hears me. Since I know that He hears me in whatever I ask, I know that I have the requests I have asked of Him

— 1 JOHN 5:14-15

And whatever I ask, I receive from Him because I keep His commandments and do what pleases Him

— 1 JOHN 3:22

I pray that the eyes of my understanding be opened to see the hope to which He has called me

— EPHESIANS 1:18

12

A PLACE TO ABIDE

"Don't expect positive changes in your Christian walk if you still abide in unbelief"

— PETER NII KORLEY

Scripture Reading:

"Abide in Me, and I in you. As the branch cannot bear fruit of itself, unless it abides in the vine, neither can you, unless you abide in Me"

— JOHN 15:4, NKJV

What It Means To Abide

The real reason that Jesus died was so we can have eternal life and dwell everlastingly with the Father, starting right here, right now. His death secured eternal life for all who believe in Him. Therefore, we are entitled to dwell everlastingly with the triune Godhead. Jesus' death on the cross paid for the sins of the world, prepared the way for us to come to the Father, and created a dwelling place for us to abide. He told the disciples that He was going to prepare a place for them (John 14: 1-6).

Since Jesus already died, rose, and is now alive forever, we know that this dwelling place has already been prepared. This chapter is meant to renew and beautify your mind to this fact so that you can find and enjoy rest in the place to abide that Jesus has prepared for you.

Abide means to wait; remain stable or fixed in a state, or continue in a place (Merriam-Webster Dictionary). Jesus said there were many dwelling places or places to abide in His Father's house (John 14:2). After preparing an abiding place for us, Jesus rose again to take us back unto Himself. He meant for us to dwell in this prepared place forever, not just after we die, but starting right here, right now. This is a place for us to abide daily and walk victoriously every single moment.

Jesus likened himself to the vine and we as the branches. The only job of the branch is to abide in or stay connected to the vine. The vine's job is to provide the right conditions and ensure that all the necessary nutrients get to the branch to produce fruit. This is why Jesus said; we can do nothing unless we abide in Him. He who abides in the dwelling place will produce fruit effortlessly.

We often try so hard to produce fruit in our lives. We work hard apart from God to try and make things happen ourselves. We look for success, victory, healing, provision, and so on outside of the place where we are supposed to abide. We end up not yielding any fruit or getting what we want. This is because we do not realize that our supply comes from the vine. The branch that stays attached to the vine does not jump off the vine to look for fruit. All the branch has to do is to stay connected to the vine to bear fruit effortlessly. So, if we remain joined to the vine, we will have all the necessary things to produce fruit effortlessly. The scriptures say, *"If you abide in Me, and My words abide in you, you will ask what you desire, and it shall be done for you"* (John 15:7, NKJV).

God Is Near

There is an inherent belief in some Christians of separation from God. They believe they are separated from God because God is in heaven while they are on earth. Their idea is that they are separated from Him now, but when they die or when Jesus comes again during the second coming, they will be with Him forever. The Bible says that Jesus ascended into heaven. So we know that Jesus is seated at the right hand of the Father right now. So we see Jesus as sitting up there while we are down here. So when we pray, we lift up our heads to heaven because we know that is where God and Jesus are.

And yes! All the above statements are true, but God invites us into a more intimate relationship than that. He wants us to remove the idea of separation from Him. He is Spirit, and we are made in His image and likeness, so we are Spirit like Him. If so, there can be no separation because there is no distance in the Spirit. The Spirit of God is one and is the same Spirit in all and sustains all. The scripture says, *"Then the LORD God formed man from the dust of the ground and breathed the breath of life into his nostrils, and the man became a living being"* (Genesis 2:7, NIV).

From the very beginning of time, the plan of God was that man should be aware of his connectedness to God and be in His presence forever. He started this plan in the Garden of Eden, but the plan got derailed through Adam and Eve's disobedience in the garden. Then God promised that through the Savior, Jesus, He would put His laws (His words) into our minds and have them written on our hearts (Hebrews 8:10) so that we could think like Him and connect with Him all the time. So, God desires that we know our oneness with Him and fellowship with Him from that place of understanding.

Scripture says that our body, as is right now, is a temple (dwelling place) for the Holy Spirit (1 Corinthians 6:19). The Spirit of God has made us, and His breath has given us life (Job 33:4). God is not far at all from any of us. In fact, He dwells inside all of us, for it is in Him we live, move, and have our being (Acts 17:28).

You must develop a consciousness of your spiritual dwelling place just like you have a consciousness of your physical dwelling. When you abide in Christ consciously, it removes the idea of separation; that is, it eliminates the concept of a God up there in the heavens apart from you. By abiding in Him, you begin to see Him as a God that is not only near but a God who dwells in you. Christ in you, the hope of glory!

Knowing Him Better

When you abide in the dwelling place Jesus has prepared, you get to know him better. He speaks to you, shows you things, helps you make better decisions, and leads you in the right path or direction for your life. You learn to recognize His thoughts, and you can easily cast down those thoughts that are not from Him.

All the answers you seek for the problems, situations, conditions, and questions that you may have exists in you right now. This is because of your union with Christ. You may not have any insight into what to do about the problem or situation you are dealing with right now. There may be no foreseeable possible solution to your issues and troubles in the natural realm at the moment, but know this: all things are possible with God (Matthew 19:26), and all things are possible with you because you believe (Mark 9:23). There is an answer to your situation. But it can only be found in the dwelling place. As you abide in Him, remain one with Him and not be moved by your circumstances, but be single-eyed about it, that is, be focused, the answer will come. You will produce fruit for His glory, and you will be a glowing testimony of His faithfulness.

We have been invited to dwell in the secret place of the Lord Most High. He did not ask us to visit this secret place occasionally or even frequently but has invited us to dwell (abide, remain) there. Scriptures say that God's dwelling place is lovely, and we should long and yearn to abide in His presence (Psalm 84:1-4). The Lord becomes a refuge and a fortress for those who decide to abide in God's secret place (Psalm 91:1-2).

Beloved, speak the affirmations below into your life, and let the Holy Spirit beautify your mind with them as you learn to dwell in His secret place.

AFFIRMATIONS FOR DWELLING PLACE

I am God's temple, and God's Spirit dwells in me

— 1 CORINTHIANS 3:16

I am not in the flesh, but in the Spirit, and the Spirit of God dwells in me

— ROMANS 8:9

In Him, I am being built together to become a dwelling in which God lives by His Spirit

— EPHESIANS 2:22

For I am God's fellow workers; I am God' field, God's building

— 1 CORINTHIANS 3:9

In Him, I live and move and have my being. I am His offspring

— ACTS 17:28

No evil shall befall me, no, sickness, plague or disease shall come near my dwelling

— PSALM 91:10

LORD, you are my dwelling place forever

— PSALM 90:1

There are many places to abide in My Father'shouse; Jesus has gone to prepare a dwelling place for me

— JOHN 14:2

Christ Jesus dwells in my heart by faith

— EPHESIANS 3:17

13

GENERAL AFFIRMATIONS

This blessed Book brings such life and health and peace, and such an abundance that we should never be poor anymore.

— SMITH WIGGLESWORTH

S cripture Reading:

"May these words of my mouth and this meditation of my heart be pleasing in your sight, LORD, my Rock and my Redeemer"

— PSALM 19:14, NIV

Why We Affirm God's Word

The Word of God is spiritual food to all of us. Just like you eat food naturally to grow, so you should feed your spirit with the Word of God to become strong spiritually. Affirming, declaring, or confessing God's Word is an integral part of the growth and development of a Christian's life.

God's Word is described as milk and as meat. The milk is for spiritual babies, while the meat of the Word of God is for the spiritually matured. New Christians and those that have not taken the time to read and meditate on God's Word so they can grow are referred to as spiritual babies. The scripture says, *I gave you milk, not solid food, for you were not yet ready for it. Indeed, you are still not ready"* (1 Corinthians 3:2, NIV).

The milk of the Word is the basic foundation or principles of faith. You have to start receiving the milk first. When you are ready, you will be able to receive the firmer meat of the Word, which is built upon the basic foundational principles. You need to start by feeding on the Word of God, putting it in your heart and your mouth, and meditating on it. Purposefully think about it, make time for it, and make it the most essential thing in your life. As you do this, you will begin to grow stronger in your spirit. The scripture says, *"As newborn babes, desire the sincere milk of the Word, that ye may grow thereby"* (1 Peter 2:2, NKJV).

The Word of God is meat or solid food for mature believers. The mature believers are those who have used God's Word to build their spiritual muscles. They have developed their faith by exercising it, just like you develop your natural muscle through exercise. The scripture says, *"But strong meat belongs to them that are of full age, even those who because of use have their senses exercised to discern both good and evil"* (Hebrews 5:14, NKJV).

When someone works very hard to build their muscles in the gym, you can tell because you can see they have a strong body. It is the same way with building up your Spirit man. After some time, one can tell what you have been feeding on, and one can see the things you are doing with your faith.

Similarly, suppose the man who used to go to the gym every day to build his muscles up gradually stops going to the gym and stops exercising his muscles. In that case, his muscles that were strong before will slowly become weaker. After a while, he will be unable to lift the kind of weights he used to lift previously and will have to work harder to restore his lost strength. This also applies to Christians who gradually stop reading, meditating, declaring, and applying the Word of God. Their spirits will become weaker, and very soon, they will not be able to stand their ground in faith and believe for the things they want anymore. Therefore, it is essential to affirm God's Word every day. Scripture says, *"The Spirit of a man will sustain his infirmity, but a wounded spirit who can bear?"* (Proverbs 18:14, KJV).

If you strengthen your spirit with the Word of God by reading, meditating, and declaring God's Word, it will sustain you through whatever comes your way and lead you on the road to victory.

GENERAL AFFIRMATIONS

For me, there is but one God, the Father, from whom all things came and for whom I live, and there is but one Lord, Jesus Christ, through whom all things came and through whom I live

— 1 CORINTHIANS 8:6

Some people trust in chariots and some others in horses, but I trust in the name of the LORD my God

— PSALM 20:7

I am blessed because I trust the LORD and have made the LORD my hope and confidence. I am just like the tree planted along a riverbank, with roots that reach deep into the water. I am not concerned about the heat or worried about long months of drought. My leaves stay green, and they never stop producing fruit

— JEREMIAH 17:7-8

Everything that belongs to Christ also belongs to me because I am an heir of God and joint-heirs with Christ

— ROMANS 8:17

I trust in the LORD for ever: for in the LORD JEHOVAH is everlasting strength

— ISAIAH 26:4

I make the secret place of the Most High my dwelling place, and I abide under the shadow of the Almighty

—PSALM 91: 1

My body is the temple of the Holy Spirit who is in me. My body belongs to God

—1 CORINTHIANS 6:19

Show me the correct path, O LORD; point out the right road for me to follow

— PSALM 25:4

The LORD is my Redeemer, the Holy One of Israel: He is my God, who teaches me what is best for me, who directs me in the way I should go

— ISAIAH 48:17

When I am afraid, I put my trust in You, my God, whose word I praise. In God, I trust, and I am not afraid

PSALM 56:3-4

God's love for me is so much that he sent Jesus to die for me so that I can have eternal life

— JOHN 3:16

God loves me as much as He loves Jesus

— JOHN 17:26

I am saved now by grace through faith in Jesus. It is not because of anything that I have done

—EPHESIANS 2:8-9

I do not owe anyone anything except to love them

—ROMANS 13:8

I obey the LORD and follow all His commands. The LORD, my God, makes me prosperous in all the work of my hands

— DEUTERONOMY 30:8-9

I am God's workmanship. I am created in Christ Jesus to do good works, which God prepared in advance for me to do

— EPHESIANS 2:10

I am not afraid because God is with me. I will not be discouraged because the Lord is my God. He will strengthen me and help me. He will hold me up with His overcoming right hand

— ISAIAH 41:10

When I pass through the waters, God will be with me; and when I go through the rivers, they will not overwhelm me. If I walk through the fire, I will not be scorched; the flames will not set me ablaze

— ISAIAH 43:2

The LORD will give me strength because I am His child; the LORD will bless me with peace

— PSALM 29:11

The spirit that I have is not of the world, but the spirit of God, that I may understand what God has freely given me

— 1 CORINTHIANS 2: 12

Christ has set me free. I stand firm, then, and do not encumber myself again with the yoke of slavery

— GALATIANS 5:1

The Spirit of God Himself bears witness with my spirit that I am a child of God

— ROMANS 8:16

Jesus has given me the power to trample on serpents and scorpions, and over all the power of the enemy. Nothing shall harm or hurt me

— LUKE 10:19

The LORD God is my sun and shield; the LORD gives me grace and glory. He does not hold back good things from me because I walk with integrity

— PSALM 84:11

No weapon forged against me will prevail. I refute every tongue that accuses me. This is my inheritance as a child of God, and my righteousness is from the Lord

— ISAIAH 54:17

I have received the abundance of grace and the gift of righteousness, and I reign in life through Jesus Christ

— ROMANS 5:17

My God is He who goes with me and fights for me against my enemies to save me

— DEUTERONOMY 20:4

The Lord fights for me, and I hold my peace

— EXODUS 14:14

The LORD is near to me because I call upon Him in truth. He fulfills my desires because I fear him; He hears my cry and saves me

— PSALM 145:18-19

The Lord causes me to abound in every good work

— 2 CORINTHIANS 9:8

I pray that the eyes of my understanding be opened to see the hope to which He has called me

— EPHESIANS 1:18

The Lord shall bless all the work of my hands so that I shall lend to many, but not borrow

— DEUTERONOMY 28:12

I seek first the Kingdom of God and His righteousness, and all the things I need are added unto me

— MATTHEW 6:33

God is my refuge and strength, my ever present help in times of trouble

— PSALM 46:1

I remember the LORD, my God, because He is the one who gives me the power to be successful

— DEUTERONOMY 8:18

I call unto the Lord, and He answers me and shows me great things that I did not know before

— JEREMIAH 33:3

REVIEWS

I sincerely hope you enjoyed reading this book as much as I enjoyed writing it. If you did, I would greatly appreciate a short review on Amazon or your favorite book website. As an independent author, reviews are crucial for me and even just a line or two can make a huge difference. I love hearing from my readers and I personally read every single review. Thank you!

Copy this url to your browser:
http://amazon.com/review/create-review
asin=1777805708

NEW BOOK

Believe Your Desires Into Your Life

God's Way

by Eunice Onode

Available on AMAZON OCTOBER 15, 2021

CONCLUSION

Now that we have come to the end of this book, I would like to reiterate some of the key concepts we learned so that even after you have closed this book, you will easily remember and apply them to your life and circumstances.

We learned in the first chapter that our identity must always be in Jesus. Deciding to follow Christ changes everything and brings you into your true identity. You become one with Christ and come to know who you really are by seeing yourself as He sees you. Your profession, achievements, physical appearance, poverty, or wealth do not define who you are. When you come to God through Jesus Christ, He becomes your identity. God loves to change people's identities so they can line up with their destinies.

God sees you as a Spirit being like He is, and God wants you to know that you too are a Spirit being just like Him. He wants you to replace the concepts that defined you before you came to know Christ with new concepts based on who God is and what He says about you. The real you (the redeemed one of Christ) is right now perfect, healed, blessed, saved, righteous, does not get discouraged, anxious, depressed, is not worried, and does not give up. The real you is exactly like God.

We learned in the second chapter that God's Word is life, gives light, produces healing, wholeness and guides us if we live according to its instructions. God speaks to us through His words, and His words reveal what God thinks about us. It reveals His character and what He plans to do. The Word of God reveals the will of God for our lives.

The Word of God can help rewire your brain and change your mindset. It will inspire you and give you the strength and wisdom you need to make your walk count for Jesus Christ. The power inherent in the Word of God can produce life and change your heart from the inside. God's Word is the only weapon that we need to combat negative mindsets, toxic thoughts and develop a beautiful mind.

When we persistently engage it by hearing, reading, meditating on it, speaking it out of our mouths, we will defeat the thoughts and the problems we face. So persistence is one of the keys to beating the enemy.

In the third chapter, we learned that we must dream big and have a God-given vision for our lives. God's Word contains God's vision which is produced when we hear the Word. The wonderful thing is that taking ownership of the vision or the picture produced by God's Word releases the faith to bring the vision to pass. So, you can stand on God's promise regarding whatever you desire to see the manifestation. When you take God's promises to heart and start seeing yourself as God sees you, you become what you see. The only way for permanent change to occur is when you agree with God's Word and begin to see the result first on the inside, which is the answer to your problems.

We learned in the fourth chapter that we must overcome negative thoughts by replacing them with God's thoughts through the power of Christ dwelling in us. Our mind is drawn to negativity, so it is so much easier to think negative thoughts, but we have to fight our minds to accept and think like God.

As sons and daughters of God, we should follow God's direction. He said we should not be anxious about anything but cast all our cares upon Him (1 Peter 5:7). Casting our cares upon Him means leaving everything in His hands and resting totally in Him.

In the fifth chapter, we learned that we are all entitled to having a well and healed body because Jesus provided for it. Jesus healed sick people in His day. The God who created our bodies is also the healer of our bodies. Jesus took your infirmities, anxieties and sicknesses, and diseases. This then implies that you no longer have them because Jesus took them. They do not belong to you anymore. Yes, illness and disease may indeed be ravaging your body in the natural, but God's Word remains true. Remember that you are in a spiritual battle for your life. The scriptures say that we are not fighting flesh and blood, so we are not engaged in a natural struggle (2 Corinthians 10:3).

Your mind will constantly draw your attention to what you see happening in your body. This is where the spiritual fight comes in. This is where you begin to cast down and negate any thoughts outside the promise of healing and health for you. However, as you continue to keep God's Word before your eyes, you will eventually enter into a state of rest in the completely finished work of Jesus on the cross, and then your healing will manifest.

We learned in the sixth chapter that the blessing is like a prepared table, and this table has everything we could ever need. We can approach the table and take what we need to overcome every situation in life. The table is always accessible by faith through Jesus Christ.

When you recognize that you have the blessing in your life, no one can put you down. You will always rise up and come out on top. The blessing in your life is of the Lord. It cannot be taken away. When you are blessed, you cannot be cursed. The blessing will bring the necessary resources and the right people to you and cause them to help you.

In the seventh chapter, we learned that expressing gratitude to God and being thankful is very essential. Thanksgiving is a way of acknowledging what God has done and is presently doing. We also thank Him for not yet manifested things because we know that God has already accomplished everything for us in the spirit.

Our gratitude should be intentional because our natural tendency is to be ungrateful. We often want to overlook the good and focus on the negative. Hence we must intentionally recognize all that we have been blessed with and consciously express our gratitude to God because gratitude pleases God.

We learned in the eighth chapter that God the Father has given all His children a measure of faith, so we all have the same amount or measure of faith. This amount of faith that we have received can be increased or decreased. The Bible says we can increase our faith by hearing God's Word (Romans 10:17). God's Word is food for our faith. Reading the Word of God every day and meditating on it all the time will help you develop your faith.

True faith believes in things larger than itself. It believes in God's promises for things and situations that are truly beyond our human ability to bring them to pass. There may be absolutely no logic to continue to believe for them, but we believe anyway. This is the secret to bringing real change to our circumstances.

We learned in chapter nine that it takes strength and courage to walk with God and follow His direction, especially when you have pressures of life coming at you from all sides while trying to make decisions. When we need help and guidance, we have the Holy Spirit to help us in every way. He teaches us God's Word and reminds us of all the promises God has given to us. God always keeps His promises. He said He would instruct us. He will tell us what steps to take and what things to avoid in order to get to our destination in life, have our needs met, or receive the answers we want.

In the tenth chapter, we learned that fear often arises from ignorance, so that we fear what we do not know or understand. The enemy of our souls usually uses our ignorance to feed and incite our imagination. Thus, he takes away our God-given vision and makes us picture things going wrong and our life situations worsening, which in turn cuts off our faith.

The vision that God gives us is filled with hope and revives our hearts. However, the vision that fear presents is full of confusion, discouragement, and hopelessness. This causes our spiritual growth to be stifled, and we begin to reverse our spiritual course. We start to hear the enemy's voice on the inside more than the voice of God, and then, we become slaves to our fears. We are never distant from God. He is always with us, so we do not need to fear. We may feel removed and distant, but that is our mind lying to us. God is near to us, and He lives in us, and we in Him, and that is the truth.

We learned in the eleventh chapter that the Lord Jesus taught us how to pray. We are to ask so that we can receive. Our prayers should be from a position of understanding our relationship with Him, as sons and daughters asking a loving Father for help. He promised to hear us when we pray and has already given us His Word to guide us so that we can pray in line with His will.

This helps us position ourselves to receive freely from Him. We must also allow our hearts to receive the answers we prayed for by seeing them and being comfortable with having them on the inside first. Then we will have it in reality.

In the twelfth chapter, 'A Place to dwell,' we reiterated how Jesus had prepared a dwelling place for us, and we dwell there by faith now. We often work hard, most times unsuccessfully, to make things work in our lives before finally turning to God as a last resort. But Jesus encouraged us to be like the branch that dwells on the vine and produces fruit effortlessly. Learning to abide in Christ removes the concept of separation from God, and we begin to see Him as a God that is not only near but a God who dwells in us. Christ in us, the hope of glory!

This book ended with some general affirmations of God's words. We talked about how God's Word can be likened to milk for spiritual babies and the unmatured in Christ while the meat of the Word is for the spiritually matured. Declaring and acting on the Word is the exercise needed to strengthen your spiritual muscles so that you can go from drinking milk to eating the meat of the Word.

We are indeed privileged to have God as our loving Father who takes care of us. His Word is so full of hope and encouragement for times of trouble. His power is made available to us through the indwelling Holy Spirit, who empowers us by reminding us of God's Word and comforting us with hope and a bright future. We have all things we need in Christ Jesus, and we can be assured that God will always work miracles in our life based on our faith and trust in Him. We are blessed to have a loving Father who truly and wonderfully cares for us.

Now that the eyes of your heart have been enlightened, I hope you will begin to use the knowledge gained from this book to deal with issues that arise in various aspects of your life. I also hope that you will start to beautify your mind with God's Word so that you can see the power of God manifest in every area of your life. God bless you!

just for you!

A FREE GIFT FOR MY READERS

Download *"How To Eliminate Negative Thoughts God's Way in 5 Simple Steps"* and start renewing your mind right away! Visit this link to get your free gift

www.euniceonode.com

REFERENCES

New International Version Bible. (2001). NIV Online.
https://www.biblestudytools.com/niv/

King James Bible. (2010). King James Bible Online.
https://www.kingjamesbibleonline.org/

New King James Bible. (2014). New King James Bible
Online. https://www.biblegateway.com/versions/New-King-
James-Version-NKJV-Bible/

Holy Bible: New Living Translation (2004). NLT Online
https://www.biblestudytools.com/nlt

Merriam-Webster.com dictionary. Merriam-Webster.https://
www.merriam-webster.com/dictionary/

Oxford English Dictionaries https://en. oxforddictionaries.com

"LEXICO Powered by OXFORD" https://www. lexico.com/en

Quotes, A. C. (2017, September 3). Pastor Mensa Otabil Quote about: #Declaration, #Life, #Situation, #Word Of God,. All Christian Quotes. https://www.allchristianquotes.org/quotes/Mensa_Otabil/5631/

Quotes, A. C. (2020, February 1). Douglas Yaw Mensah Quote about: #God, #Favor, #Opportunities, #World,. All Christian Quotes. https://www.allchristianquotes.org/quotes/Douglas_Yaw_Mensah/13544/

Quotes, A. C. (2020b, March 31). Ronnie (Ron) Millevo Quote about: #Believe, #Faith, #Coronavirus, #Damage,. All Christian Quotes. https://www.allchristianquotes.org/quotes/Ronnie_Ron_Millevo/13635/

Quotes, A. C. (2020a, January 14). Arome Osayi Quote about: #Man, #Prayer, #Faith, #Pray,. All Christian Quotes. https://www.allchristianquotes.org/quotes/Arome_Osayi/13286/

Quotes, A. C. (2020c, February 21). Peter Nii Korley Quote

about: #Life, #Follow, #Daily, All Christian Quotes. https://
www.allchristianquotes.org/quotes/Peter_Nii_Korley/13608/

Quotes, A. C. (1968). 120 Christian Quotes & Sayings by
Kenneth E Hagin (Quotations). All Christian Quotes. https://
www.allchristianquotes.org/authors/137/Kenneth_E_Hagin/

Quotes, A. C. (1968). 133 Christian Quotes & Sayings by Martin
Luther King Jr (Quotations). All Christian Quotes. https://www.
allchristianquotes.org/authors/198/Martin_Luther_King_Jr/

Quotes, A. C. (1975). 111 Christian Quotes & Sayings by Smith
Wigglesworth (Quotations). All Christian Quotes. https://
www.allchristianquotes.org/authors/22/Smith_Wigglesworth/

Quotes, A. C. (2017a, January 9). Benson Andrew Idahosa
Quote about: #Fear, #God, #Side, #Worry,. All Christian
Quotes. https://www.allchristianquotes.org/quotes/
Benson_Andrew_Idahosa/201/

Quotes, A. C. (2017b, January 15). David O. Oyedepo Quote
about: #Yourself, #Worrying, #Put, #Dependence,. All Christian
Quotes. https://www.allchristianquotes.org/quotes/
David_O_Oyedepo/789/

Quotes, A. C. (2018, May 30). Victoria Osteen Quote about:

#Complain, #Gratitude, #People, #Practice,. All Christian
Quotes. https://www.allchristianquotes.org/quotes/
Victoria_Osteen/12207/

Quotes, A. C. (2017c, January 22). Rod Parsley Quote about:
#Jesus Christ, #Everything, #Health, #Difficulties,. All Christian
Quotes. https://www.allchristianquotes.org/quotes/
Rod_Parsley/1582/

Quotes, A. C. (2017d, April 7). Mark Driscoll Quote about:
#Christ, #Joy, #Suffering, #Inactivity,. All Christian Quotes.
https://www.allchristianquotes.org/quotes/
Mark_Driscoll/4011/

Made in the USA
Monee, IL
05 March 2023

29226403R00111